Inside Kenya – Creating Tomorrow
Stories of Twelve Extraordinary Kenyan Lives

Each of us can make a
difference in worlds faraway.

Sandra Harper

Sandra Harper

Hawthorne Publishing Company

National Library of Canada Cataloguing in Publication Data

Inside Kenya, creating tomorrow: stories of twelve extraordinary Kenyan lives/
Sandra Harper

Includes bibliographical reference

ISBN: 0-9734986-1-7

    1. Educational assistance, Canadian – Kenyan
    2. Continuing education – Kenya I. Title

DT433.582.A2H37 2005   374.96762   C2005-900707-9

Although the author and publisher have made every effort to ensure the
accuracy and completeness of information about the twelve individuals,
the organizations, and the country of Kenya in this book, we assume no
responsibility for errors, inaccuracies, omissions, or any inconsistency within.

Edited by James Young
Cover Photograph by Jay Procktor
Cover Design by Shirley Olson
Text Design by Shirley Olson
Printing by Transcontinental Printing
Photographs by Sandra Harper, Jay Procktor,
Maureen McDonald and Wayne Crossen

www.hawthornepublishing.com
Printed and Bound in Canada

Foreward

FROM PETER N.R.O. OGEGO,

KENYAN HIGH COMMISSIONER, OTTAWA

INSIDE KENYA – CREATING TOMORROW: STORIES OF TWELVE EXTRAORDINARY KENYAN LIVES, by Dr. Sandra Harper, provides good examples of how change can be spurred through focused philanthropic interventions or charitable causes, however modest, in poverty-stricken communities. In this easy-to-read self-renditions of how the lives of twelve young Kenyans, born in abject poverty, have changed through the provision of education study-grants by Canadian N.G.O.s, CHES and ACCES, Dr. Sandra not only inspires fellow Canadians to rise up to what Canadians are globally-known for—charity and compassion—and replicate these efforts, but she also gives hope and encouragement to those many youths found in communities in Africa that, with sustained education, they can create their tomorrow.

It is noteworthy that in the beginning 2003, Kenya Government put education as its top priority and adopted a policy of free, compulsory primary education for all children of school going age. The Government is also giving due consideration to the possibility of extending the free or subsided education policy to cover secondary school and university levels. In the meantime, however, efforts by volunteer and charitable N.G.O.s such as CHES and ACCES are highly appreciated and will always be supported by the authorities.

I highly recommend reading INSIDE KENYA – CREATING TOMORROW: STORIES OF TWELVE EXTRAORDINARY KENYAN LIVES for those Canadians and any other volunteers and philanthropists who wish to make a difference in the lives of people who still live under poverty in the developing world.

For my grandchildren—Dean Robyn,
Kaylen, Kelsey and Matthew—
Who always inspire.
And for Beth and George Scott,
Who made a dream into reality for so
many people.

Also by Sandra Harper

Traveling the Sun: A Healing Journey In Morocco, Tunisia and Spain

This Book Is Dedicated to......

....All the young men and women of Kakamega, Kenya, whose lives have been changed by the A.C.C.E.S. support of their education.

....The twelve Kenyans: Cappitus, Connie, Davis, Elisha, Everlyne, Florence, Francis Godfrey, Justine, Margaret, Philip, and Whycliffe who shared their stories with me. Each of them spoke with honesty and openness about his or her life. The deep appreciation and respect with which they held both A.C.C.E.S. and CHES—two Canadian organizations that funded their education—was evident in their words and actions. I found great joy in getting to know these men and women and recognize their potential for making a difference in Kenya.

....Beth and George Scott whose support and encouragement made this book possible.

....The accomplishments of A.C.C.E.S. in supporting the education of young Kenyans at post-secondary schools and of children at the primary literacy centers in the rural areas of Kakamega, Kenya.

....The long-term commitment of CHES to provide funding for poor, intellectually capable secondary students.

....James Young for his perceptive and thorough editing which helped to shape each story.

....Charlotte Gauttchau, Alice Tiles and Anne Low for their reading of the next-to-final draft and their constructive feedback.

....Juhli Fox who read the final draft of this book with thoroughness and care.

....Jay Procktor who provided the stunning photographs for the cover and individual pages.

....Wayne Crossen and Maureen MacDonald for their excellent photographs of Kenyan life that helped to provide a visual glimpse into Kenya.

....My writing group: Betty Carter, Catherine Hawthorne, Linda Negrave, Marilyn Grant, Mary Anne Pare, and Joan Vieira, who listened to my original drafts. They encouraged me and suggested changes that made my writing the best it could be.

....And finally to my grandchildren with love: Dean and Robyn Massecar; Kaylen, Kelsey and Mathew VanSickle, who are the tomorrows of our family.

Contents

Starting a New Tomorrow

*E*xcitement burned deep within me when I arrived in Kenya as an A.C.C.E.S. volunteer. I knew that I wanted to assist A.C.C.E.S., the African Canadian Continuing Education Society. It is an organization based in British Columbia which has been working in Western Kenya since 1993 to educate youth and teachers. I thought about the images that the North American media promotes about Africa—starving children, battered people walking from a calamity or war, white people giving food and dollars to help Africans survive. What I saw in Kenya was different. Kenya is not just a country of people dying from AIDS and lack of food. Everyday I saw men and women working in stores, restaurants and *duchas*—huts in the markets and along the streets. I watched nurses and doctors looking after patients; taxi-drivers, and *boda-boda* drivers bicycling people around the town; teachers helping children in schools; and families looking after crops and cattle on their small farms.

For six months in 2003, I lived as a volunteer in Kakamega, located in the Western Province of Kenya. My life mingled with the Luyha people of this area. I became part of the region of Kenya that has the most poverty, the highest unemployment and one of the highest illiteracy rates in the country. Half of the residents of Kakamega District live below the poverty line. Unemployment rate in Western Province ranges around fifty percent. Only forty-two percent of the children go to Primary School, which is the same as the elementary grades one to eight in Canada. In today's world the most important challenge for Kenyans is to bring about change to create a new tomorrow.

I was attracted to come as a volunteer in Kenya for several reasons. I had retired as an elementary school principal and was widely travelled. The death of my eldest son from leukemia had left me searching out how to make a difference in my own life. I had explored Northern Africa, but the rest of the continent was new territory. Then, from a friend, I heard about this small Canadian organization, A.CC.E.S, who needed volunteers to assist in Kakamega.

A.C.C.E.S. is one of two Canadian development organizations working in Kakamega, the capital city of the Western Province, to foster social and economical development through education. Founded in 1993 by Beth and George Scott, British Columbian retirees, the belief that drives this small organization is that Kenyan youth, through education, can begin to bring about change in their country and develop a sense of self-reliance in their communities.

To turn that belief into reality, the Scott's encouraged ordinary Canadians to donate money towards A.C.C.E.S. scholarships for bright, but needy, young men and women to complete post-secondary studies at universities, colleges and trade schools. Many of the poor, high achieving secondary students that they considered for scholarships had received secondary school scholarship from another Canadian organization, called CHES. Over 600 men and women from Kakamega, Kenya, have successfully completed their post-secondary degrees and programs to the present time from A.C.C.E.S. scholarship donations.

Every day, in Kakamega, I met with young and old Kenyans in need. I also encountered men and women, educated through the support of A.C.C.E.S. scholarships, who had emerged from the cocoon of poverty, found in peasant farming families, into self-sufficient professional people needed for the modern world of Kenya. These ordinary Kenyans were leading extraordinary lives. I found that each person, in being helped by a Canadian scholarship, was now helping other Kenyans to be educated. A circle of change has started.

Seeing the difference that A.C.C.E.S. was making, I was driven to develop an awareness in Canadians and people in other countries about the face of poverty in today's Kenya—to tell the stories of some ordinary lives of rural Kenya and what happens when their children are educated. Through sustained education, ordinary Kenyans are being equipped to make a difference inside modern Kenya. Ordinary people can create their tomorrow.

I selected the twelve men and women, A.C.C.E.S. graduates, in different ways. Beginning with Everlyne, Francis, and Florence who worked with A.C.C.E.S. Kenya, I ended in Nairobi with Alisha and Cappitus whom I had heard so much about from others. I observed their lives, sat in meetings with them, sipped milk-tea with individuals, and listened through a series of very candid interviews. As these opportunities opened, each man and woman became more familiar to me. I began to understand their personal backgrounds, ambitions, longings, drives, and personal characteristics that pushed them to be educated and then to become successful. Each of these twelve Kenyans is excited that the proceeds from the sale of their stories will go into the A.C.C.E.S. Scholarship Fund to assist other young Kenyans to have a post-secondary education.

Inside Kenya – Creating Tomorrow: Stories of Twelve Extraordinary Kenyan Lives is an anthology of men and women whose accounts need to be read. Their stories will give you the opportunity to explore the lives of today's Kenyans that are different from your own, yet somewhat hauntingly familiar. Each of them shows how one small Canadian organization, A.C.C.E.S., has developed, through education, Kenyans who are professionals involved in their own country. Enter their world— in making a difference inside Kenya.

A Little Bit of History

*I*n reading IN KENYA – CREATING TOMORROW, two Canadian organizations—A.C.C.E.S. and CHES—are mentioned time and time again. Readers might be interested in a short description about how these two organizations came to Kenya.

In Kenya, students who go to secondary schools and then post-secondary educational institutions must pay all costs: tuition fees to attend courses, textbooks, uniforms, classroom supplies, examinations, tutoring, release of examination results, extra-curricular activities, and transportation costs are only some of the requirements. These fees make it impossible for most children from poor farming families to attend any school.

In the early 1980's, Lorrie Williams, a Canadian teacher from New Westminster, came to Kakamega, in the Western Province of Kenya, to teach as a volunteer in a secondary school. In 1982, she started CHES and began to pay the secondary school tuition fees for a few individual students. When she returned to Canada she set up, in 1985, a formal N.G.O. organization, Canadian Harambee Education Society, commonly known as CHES. Its purpose was to seek Canadian donors to fund scholarships for the poor, but bright boys and girls to go to secondary school. A *harambee*, in Kenya, is when people gather together to give money to an individual to help meet his or her educational or medical goals. CHES has received annual donations from Canadians to support hundreds students in Kakamega Secondary Schools over the past twenty years.

In 1995, CHES moved to funding only females in secondary school. This change came about as Canadian volunteers began to gradually understand Kenyan culture. A poor family who had very little money normally selected the sons to go to school because it was believed that they would get jobs and support the entire family. In peasant families, the role of females was to marry, produce children and look after the farming. In addition, when a girl was sent to school by her family she was still expected to do all the women's work before and after school. These tasks were so time-consuming that girls were left with little time to study and complete school assignments, causing girls and young women to rarely achieve above the average level. With this change to providing scholarships to girls only, CHES sought to support more girls going into secondary school.

5

In 1992, Beth and George Scott, recent retirees from Surrey, British Columbia, visited Kakamega, Kenya. After they saw the positive impact CHES had accomplished in getting students from very poor families into secondary school, Beth and George recognized the need to continue the financial support of these young men and women so they could go on to post-secondary education.

They set up, in 1993, a sister organization called A.C.C.E.S.—African Canadian Continuing Education Society. Its purpose was to continue the financial support of these young men and women so that they could go on to universities, colleges, nursing schools, and trade skills institutes. A.C.C.E.S. based their organization on the vision that education of young adults would provide Kenyans with the skills to bring about change in their country. To date over six hundred young men and women have been funded to attend post-secondary educational institutions by individual Canadian A.C.C.E.S. donors. Presently, these scholarships are provided to some CHES students and to other high achieving, poor students who are recommended or apply themselves to A.C.C.E.S.

Some graduates, like the ones described in this book have gone on to provide financial support for their brothers and sisters' education. Other graduates talk about the need to set up foundations to give funds for the education of the poor and needy in Kenya. These Kenyans recognize that education will help to change and improve their society. Having been helped by Canadians, these men and women want to assist others.

Given this background of how Canadians have helped to support the education of a number of young men and women in Kakamega, readers can now turn the pages to learn about twelve ordinary Kenyans from poor peasant backgrounds who have achieved extraordinary accomplishments by their own efforts and the assistance of A.C.C.E.S. scholarships. Through education, each of them moulds their tomorrow.

PHOTO COURTESY JAY PROCKTOR

▓ *Whycliffe Kibusu*

A short man, about five foot, five inches tall, strides into the living room in Tsimba House. A smile lights up his dark eyes as he comes over to give my hand a firm shake.

He sits down and eagerly accepts a glass of water. The drive from Mumias has been hot and dry.

At 26 years of age, Wycliffe has become a successful accountant, working at the large Mumias Sugar Company. He earns a good salary and lives in a spacious house on the company's estate, with access to the estate's club, swimming pool and golf course.

After he gets himself comfortable, Whycliffe looks out the window towards sun-glossed magenta bougainvillaea flowers climbing up the opposite wall. He begins his story in a soft, gentle voice.

"I was born in 1975 in the Kakamega District—in the rural area, close to a tiny village called Igunga, somewhere between here and Kisumu. A world that is so different from my present times. My Mother and Father never went to school. I was the fourth-born child. I had four sisters, two brothers, and one step-brother that didn't live with us. The nine of us lived in a traditional thatched house, but most of the grass had been pulled off the roof. Each night, we put our mattress on the mud floor that we had smeared by hand with cow dung to prevent jiggers and other bugs from feasting on us. Instead of one large mattress, we laid down a rug made from an old gunny bag, torn into strips and sewn together. On top of this, we each put down a maize sack, the kind used to pack the maize, corn kernels, to the market. This became our bed and we snuggled together, like forks and spoons, to keep warm during the chill of the long nights. When it rained, the water drops fell on us and woke us up. We got up, shifting our bedding so it did not get wet and, of course, so we did not get drenched. Since it rains nearly every evening in this part of Kenya, moving our bedding was a frequent activity during the dark nights. We followed the same procedure when army worms attacked us during the Long Rains season. Sleep often became difficult because it was disturbed so frequently.

When I was young, my Father worked on the tea estates, in the hills near Kericho—quite a distance from where we lived, higher in the mountains. You know Kakamega is at a 5,000 foot altitude and tea grows well in even higher places. That's where he was. He toiled picking the tea leaves in the hot day's sun. In the evenings, a white person trained him to repair and make radios. Occasionally, my Mother visited him at the tea estate, but basically she was a single parent. She bore all the work of raising her seven children while she farmed the quarter-acre of land we had from my Father's family. She grew successive crops of *sukuma*, that dark green leafy vegetable, like bitter spinach, that we used to make *sukuma wiki,* which is just boiled *sukuma*. We used it to accompany the cooked, ground maize, called *ugali*. I helped my Mother by digging the soil because my three older sisters got married very young—before they were fourteen. Only my younger brothers and my little sister were at home with my Mother and me while I was growing up.

I joined a nursery school at Igunga when I was six years of age. I repeated the first year because we couldn't raise 100 Shillings, about $1.50 Canadian, to pay for the certificate. We had to pay for everything at school: from test-taking to uniforms and extra-curricular activities that we had to participate in. As a very young child, I believed that I couldn't go to public school because we couldn't pay the school fees. Many children, especially from the rural areas did not have the opportunity for education because their parents had no money. However, in 1982, I joined Standard One at Igunga Primary School. I don't know where the money came from to pay the fees, but I do remember during the first two terms I never went to school because I was very ill with some chronic disease. I don't know what it was, but I spent seven months in hospital.

When I came home and started school again, I wrote the exams of term three only. You know, in Kenya, that even six year olds must pass these exams before they can pass to the next level. I had not completed the tests from the other terms, but I went into Standard Two by my own wits. The teacher of my Standard One class was a man who drank all day. On the last day of school he called out the names of students who had not passed the examinations.

"Those students whose names have not been called out are to go to Standard Two," he then announced,

I simply followed his directions and went to Standard Two. In fact, I found out later my name was not on any list. I guess it was at that point that I realized if I wanted to get ahead I was going to have to be smart and seek the opportunities myself. A good thing to know before I was seven years old.

In Standard Two, my health was back on track. In the morning I would go to school. In the late afternoon and early evenings I worked on our farm. On weekends we sold bananas and *sukuma* on the side of the road by our house. Even with all my time and efforts spent to help my Mother, I started to excel at school. I achieved fourteenth place in our Standard Two class. When I told my Mother the good news about my achievement, she was not encouraging or proud.

"Whycliffe, why can't you be number one?" she said harshly. "You can't be in my house if you continue to be fourteenth."

I gave her excuses, but her firm expectation gave me the motivation to excel. She wanted me in first place because she believed I was smart enough to master the subjects. Perhaps she also saw me as her only hope for the future. With high marks, I could go to college or university and get a job. Then I would support her.

In the second term of Standard Two I applied myself seriously to my studies and examinations. I earned the number three spot. The first place was taken by our neighbour's son. My Mother did not lessen her pressure.

"The neighbour boy is no better than you," she said. "Juma, his father, pushes Walter to succeed because he found that education had opened doors for him. Being educated made it possible for Juma to teach at the university. You see how he got ahead and out of this poverty we are mired in. Education is the way. Now you must do better to get us a different life."

By term three, I had reached the number one spot and my Mother's response still pushed me to pursue excellence. "Whycliffe, you are going to be in the same class as Walter next term. You have shown that you are as smart as he is. Now you must be number one all this year at school."

I did maintain my spot as the eight-year old king of the academic pile. However, in Standard Four, Father returned home with no job and no money. There were many arguments between my parents. He wanted all the money we made from the sale of the *sukuma* and bananas, but Mother hid the money she earned. I never asked where her secret place was because I was afraid Father would try to beat it out of me. His hand was always heavy on me for any little infraction—the wrong tone in my voice or arriving late at home from school simply set him off.

Anyway, Mother had all kinds of ruses to make Father believe she had no money. Early each morning she sent me to the shops for tea and sugar. I don't know what she told Father. Perhaps that I was borrowing them from neighbours in the village. When I returned I had to make tea for my brothers and sister. Because of these chores I started to leave later for school. Soon I arrived late for every class. It was then I felt the teacher stopped liking me. I believed she thought I was just a very poor and dirty child who had a Father that spent all his money on drinking. I remember, even more, that my clothes were tattered because sometimes I used thorns to hold them together. I can see now that the situation affected me psychologically. Regardless of my inner and family turmoil, I continued to go to school because it was a safe and stimulating place to be.

In Standard Four, when I was nine, my world turned black. My teachers hated me. My Father hated me. All the students in my class hated me. I was beat up because I was very small for my age and I couldn't fight back. I guess the lack of food prevented normal growth. By the end of term one, my standing in the examinations had dropped back down to number fourteen. I was shattered. I was failing at the only place where I wanted to be. In term two, I stayed in our house and refused to go to school or outside to play. The neighbour kids laughed at me all the time. I could hear them laughing and joking while I was in our *banda*, our hut. I knew they didn't like me.

"You don't have any texts or notebooks," they continually taunted me.

"One day you will be successful," my Mother said in a new manner to me. "I know you will be," as she put her arms around me. "Now, do what you can. Try to do as much as you can."

I went back to school eventually, but my Father continued to torment me. At night, when I was doing my school assignments in the light of a lantern at the table, he would turn the lantern off and tell me to cook supper. My Mother could not intervene since this would result into a fight. So I had to bear the harassment. After Father put out the lantern, I wrote by the light of the cooking fire's ashes. I remember my frustration at not having an eraser to make changes in my written compositions. The only thing that kept me going was the encouragement my Mother gave me.

In term two, one event happened in a Math class at school that turned my life around. The teacher had written columns of numbers on a wall that had been painted black to be our blackboard. The teacher called on one of the bright boys to come to the wall and add up one column of double digit numbers.

"Has he got this sum right?" he asked us.

Everyone, but me, called out, "Yes," and shot their hands up. I knew my classmates had made an error, so I did not lift my hand.

"What is wrong with this guy?" the teacher said, pointing at me. "Is there anyone who thinks he didn't get the right answer?"

I raised my arm high in the air. Immediately the teacher asked me to come to the front and do the sum.

"Yes, this is correct. Go sit down now. The rest of you must be punished to teach you to add your sums more carefully. All of you, but Whycliffe, must stay in at lunch time and complete this new page of sums."

This simple and brief event caused the students to develop a real interest in me. They began to bring me their difficult sums to do. As a payback, I could use their textbooks since I didn't have enough money to buy my own. For some students, I did their entire assignments and they gave me notebooks, pencils, occasionally a textbook and money. The teacher, who did not know about my moonlighting activities, made me the Class Perfect and the Class Monitor. My marks began to pick up and, by the end of term two, I was back in first place. There were some fluctuations in Standards Five, Six, and Seven. My marks dropped because of the negative attitude that some new teachers had towards me. But a more important event pushed me even further downward.

During Standard Six, I fell, head-first from a tree, and was hospitalized for five months in Kakamega General Hospital. My head was swollen, but the doctors said that they couldn't do an operation. Of course, I missed all those classes while I was injured and in hospital. When I came back to school, I didn't do well on the examinations, but I was placed in Standard Seven. The next year, at the end of the first term of Standard Eight, I placed fourth in academic standings—right back to my position at the beginning of Standard Five. I guess that head injury didn't destroy too many of my brain cells. In the second and third terms, I moved to third position. During this time my Mother was very ill, but she always encouraged me everyday to do the best that I could do. She never stopped thinking about me, no matter how sick she felt. She made me feel so loved.

However, my Father was a completely different type of parent. Father now had a cleaner's job at Chavakali Secondary School, earning 500 Shillings per month, and he also earned money by repairing radios. When he came home he yelled at me that he would not pay my fees because I was smoking opium. I couldn't understand where he got that idea. My Father paid my young sister's and brother's Standard Four fees for secondary school, but continued to refuse to fund me to write the necessary tests to complete primary school. He knew I was going to do very well at secondary school. I believed that because he did not have the money to pay for my high school education, he must have been very embarrassed. If he did not pay for the primary school's final exams, then I would not progress to secondary school and the others in the community wouldn't know that he couldn't pay for my education. But, without telling him, my Mother gave me money that she had saved to pay for my final exams at primary school. Until a student paid, he or she could not graduate from primary school and be assigned a secondary school. In Kenya, the Department of Education assigned each student to a specific secondary school, depending on his marks.

My home situation continued to be difficult. My Father came home drunk nearly every day. He always challenged me to excel in Science, like I did in Mathematics. Father had never gone to school, but he was bright. So was my Mother. She was good in figuring out Math problems and equations in her head. She learned to write her name at some class while I was in Primary School. I realized, as a child, she had potential for learning; she just never had the opportunity. Poverty plagued her childhood, just as it continued with her children.

Our family was so poor that I wore the same shorts everyday to school from Standard Four to Standard Eight. These shorts were covered with patches. When I was set to write my National Primary examinations, my Dad brought shorts for me from the school where he worked. He had been given a gift of money by one of the students who had passed Form Four at Chavakali. The shorts were too big for me. On the day of my exams my Mother instructed me not to wear the new shorts since I had managed for five years with the old ones. She said that this was where my luck was and I had to do my exams wearing my old shorts. My Father, for the first time, agreed with my Mother's decision. I can still remember him telling me something that I couldn't believe my ears were hearing.

"Just go and do you exams today. Do well," he pronounced as he stood in the doorway as I put on my usual old shorts.

I was amazed at his turnabout and so I could only nod my head as I dashed out the door.

After I finished writing the tests, I felt that I had not done well. The stress of whether I was going to get money to pay for the examinations had ground down my enthusiasm for studying and preparation. At the same time, my Mother continued to be unwell. The doctor couldn't explain her illness. In a whispery voice, one evening, Mother told me that she had been poisoned by her brother-in-law's wife because they believed that she was making a lot of money in the sales of the vegetables she raised. My Father's family thought she had taken over her husband's property and was farming it to make a profit. Mother had kept quiet because she didn't want wars in the family. She explained she had been given roast meat, just awhile ago, by her sister-in-law who had always said she would kill her. In ignorance Mother consumed the meat. She advised me to keep away from the farm until I had succeeded in finishing my schooling and had a job. Then I was to look for land elsewhere. Mother knew she was going to die, and she didn't want me to fall into the same trap.

During her illness, I took over caring for the family. I did the farming and cooked for my Mother, both breakfast and dinner, whenever Father could get some food. It reached a point that I could not move or change her. My Mother was completely bed-ridden at home. In Kenyan culture a male is not allowed to change a woman's clothes or to care for her when she is ill. I contacted one of my older sisters and asked her to come and help. She arrived in three days and took over caring for our Mother.

For a month after the exams I wouldn't check my results. One evening my Mother called me to her bed and softly murmured to me that I should go and see what my results were.

"I am very ill from these poisons and I am not sure how much longer I will live. I don't want to die without knowing what you achieved. If you did not score high enough, then you must go to stay with my brother and learn to be a carpenter. With that skill, you will be able to support yourself and your brothers and sister."

I couldn't believe what my Mother was saying. My Uncle was a man who had never given me a cent in his life. I felt that I couldn't survive without my Mother's guidance and encouragement. I decided then and there I must go into the village and find my test results. As I walked into our village, a rich lady congratulated me for my results and gave me 100 Shillings.

"Go and see what you got on the test," she exclaimed. "You and your family are going to be so happy. You got ninety-eight percent in Mathematics."

As I was walking towards the school, people pointed at me. I was very uneasy with this attention. I used the bush path so people couldn't see me. I came out of the trees and shrubs just before the school. I walked over to the school's door where the examination results were posted. I looked for my name and quickly I found it at the top of the list. I was by far the best student. I was one of the top three Mathematics students in the whole country. I had achieved 98/100—the first student in our school to ever have done that. It was a record-breaking achievement. I was now assured I would go onto a very good secondary school. A high mark like this guaranteed I would be called to the best school. And, just moments ago, I had been thinking the only thing that would be happening to me was I would live with my Uncle to learn to use carpentry tools.

When I was striding home in our village, another very old Mama, which a Kenyan term of endearment for women, called out to me.

"I heard you did well. My sister knows someone who will help you. In fact, my daughter works for a foreigners' organization, called CHES, that assists poor, bright students go to secondary school."

"That would help me now when I most need the money to go to secondary school," I said as I walked over to her. "Come over and talk to my Mother. She is ill, but she will see you about this matter."

The old lady came that afternoon to our house and she told my Mother about this Canadian organization. My Mother refused to allow the lady to take me to CHES and she gave no reason.

However, as I walked the woman outside, she said, "Come on Friday to see me." She reached into her pouch under her blouse and gave me 50 Shillings.

"No, I can't take your money. Why do you want to help me?"

"If you don't go to CHES my friend won't believe or trust me. She wanted me to help her find needy, in fact the poorest, students who would do very well at school. You obviously can do that. All you have to do is go to visit the lady at CHES."

I refused her offer since my Mother had declined also. I didn't want to upset my Mother. When my Father came in that evening, an older teacher, from far away, came to our hut with a message from the old woman. For some reason, Father decided to go to listen to what the lady had to say that night. I was on edge because I didn't know what was going to happen. After the lady told him about the scholarship, she explained the directions to my Father and gave him the fare for the two of us to go the CHES office by *matatu*.

My Father just said to me he understood the information and would think about it. Darkness came in a few moments and it was time for us to go to bed. For hours, my Father tossed and turned. Near dawn, I could see him begin to doze by the fire. After an hour or so I could hear his snoring so I knew he was in deep sleep. I couldn't sleep at all. I just thought about my life and my Mother. I realized that my Father was affected by my Mother's illness, as well as what to do about the scholarship. I knew he had promised my Mother that he would never remarry if anything happened to her.

Early Friday I prepared to go to Kakamega. My Father announced he would come with me. We caught the *matatu* to Kakamega and asked the direction to the teacher's house. When we arrived she decided that she would come with us and led us to the CHES office in Matende Secondary School. We knocked on the door and the CHES agent invited us in. The teacher talked to the Canadian lady for us because neither my father nor I felt we could speak English well enough. Because I was poor and had scored so high on the provincial examination, the Agent awarded me a scholarship immediately. Then she took us shopping to get my uniform, shoes, textbooks, school supplies. And a school bag— the first one I had ever had. This introduction to CHES was the most important turning point in my life. I truly am grateful to the old lady who took the initiative to tell me about CHES.

The following Monday, I started Chavakali Boarding School. It seemed strange to me that I would be attending the school where my Father worked at as a cleaner. I dreaded leaving my Mother. She had become very ill over that momentous weekend. In the first term I didn't do well because I thought always of my Mother.

In the first term of the second year, I was called to the hospital in Kakamega. My Mother was critically ill. I rushed to her side. In a faraway, faint voice she said she had some things to tell me so that I would understand what had happened and never forget. I bend my ear close to her mouth as she murmured.

"You know your Dad was a stepson in his family. He was born to your Grandfather's second wife. His stepbrothers, from your Grandfather's first wife, thought that, when we married, I made your Father take a part of the family's land. Over the years, your Father's family has tried to make me leave our property. That is why I stayed with you kids on the farm when your Father went to work on the tea estates in Kericho. Your Uncle and his wife gave me some chameleon meat with a slow poison in it. It has caused this horrible illness. I know now that I will not live much longer. I cannot stay—even though I want to see you graduate. Your Father is at the end of his ropes and will not survive for long after I die. He is a drunkard and cannot break the hold alcohol has on his life. But it is me, I know, that the family saw as a threat. What I want you to promise me is that you will take care of your brothers and sister. Keep away from the evil ones in our family, and don't show them any hatred. My sister and her husband in Nairobi will be there if you need help."

She kissed my hand and closed her eyes. Tears streamed from my eyes onto her blue blanket. I stood there for minutes, hours, days. I can't recall the length of time. All I know is time stood still.

A short time later, on the day after my birthday, my Mother died. I was devastated. I don't celebrate my birthday to this present day because the memories of that day hurl pain into my heart.

After Mother's death, my Father's attitude towards me changed. Although he was still drinking heavily everyday, he brought me some money while I was at high school. He also shared with me that he had promised my Mother that he wouldn't marry any other wife.

Because there was no Mother to be interested in their education, my younger brothers dropped out of school and made *Chang'Aa,* a liquor made from maize, to sell. One of them drank too much *Chang 'Aa* and smoked *banga*—something like marijuana. My youngest sister went down an even worse road. Her behaviour turned wild. She was caught stealing and arrested. I came over from the secondary school to talk with each of them because my Dad was not dealing with them at all.

When I finished secondary school, my Aunt, who did not have any children, called me to come to Nairobi for a month's break. I took the nine-hour bus ride into that big, sprawling capital city and found my way to the apartment of my Aunt and Uncle. When they heard what was happening to my sister, my Uncle was insistent I go back to our village and bring my sister to their home. My Aunt emphatically stated she had a duty to look after her dead sister's daughter. I took the bus back and picked up my sister to return to their home.

After we settled in, my Aunt sent my sister to a community school. She told her she had to change her behaviours and develop a positive attitude within one month. Otherwise she would be sent back home to Igunga. My sister accepted this decision without a fight, which surprised and amazed me. I suppose her behaviour was all the result of having no Mother, and a Father that couldn't cope, even with his own life. Once the month was up, my Aunt and Uncle said that my sister and I could stay for the entire time of my two-year gap period between secondary school and university. To earn money I bought and sold *sukuma* in a market. My sister pitched in and helped me. I started to like her again and to recognize her good qualities. All that year, my Aunt showed her belief in my sister by never locking a room in their apartment, even her bedroom where she kept her money. Within a year my sister had reformed her behaviour. She even gave me some of the money she was earning for my university expenses. Our belief in her basic goodness carried her from the pits of despair into the light of hope.

The results of the secondary school final examinations were announced. My Aunt told me to go back to Chavakali and pick up my results

"You are among the 6,000 who will go to university," she said excitedly.

"No, I don't think I did any better than a C," I replied.

On the bus back to Chavakali, one of the students congratulated me and said Mr. Chigala was planning a party for me. Mr. Chigala was a man in our village who had married a Canadian and they used to go to the CHES meetings. The student told me Mr. Chigali saw my results and came to my home, but I wasn't there. Even so, he decided he would hold a celebration for me. Of course with that information, I was very eager to see my marks. I stopped at the school, I ran up to the marks board and found my name. I achieved an A minus and was one of the top four students. I jumped up and down like a banshee and shouted great bellows of excitement.

Mr. Chigala organized the big party for me and invited many people, including the CHES and A.C.C.E.S. Agents. A.C.C.E.S. had started in Kakamega in 1993. They provided scholarships to high achieving, poor students to go to university or college and gave preference to students who had graduated from secondary school with high marks on a CHES scholarship. Mr. Chiagala announced at the party that I was the first person from our Igunga Primary School to get the opportunity to go to university.

I believed I would like to study medicine at the university. After careful thought and with a sudden realization that I couldn't stand to see dead bodies, I decided against that course of study. My Aunt and Mr. Chigala recommended that I go into a Bachelor of Commerce because of my strength in Mathematics. It was a four-year programme. They told me that when I completed that programme, I could come back, get a job and help my family because they did not have anyone else. I decided on a Commerce degree and was delighted to receive an A.C.C.E.S. scholarship.

However, I found my first year at the University of Nairobi horrible. In the Commerce facility, most students had already taken their C.P.A., Certified Public Accountancy, course at college. They all knew each other. When one of them asked me if I had done my C.P.A., I didn't know what he was referring to. When I asked my Uncle, he thought it was some kind of drink. I definitely felt the odd one out. I decided to do something about it. I studied and sat for the Certified Public Accountancy exams while I was completing my Bachelor of Commerce.

At the beginning of the year, the lecturer of our class of two hundred and fifty students, announced to us,

"Half of you are wasting your time here. You should be helping your Grandmothers at home. There has never been a first class in the Accounting option of our Bachelor of Commerce programme. First class is for gods alone."

I took that remark as a personal challenge and I started to work very hard. To cope with the exclusion I felt from my fellow students, I studied during my out-of-class time and did not get involved in any social activities. It paid off. The other students knew I was doing well. Some of them asked me to coach them on the course content. In return, I asked them to buy food for me. That helped me survive on my scholarship funds.

I continued to support my Father who was still at home and was now very sick. I skipped lunches to save money to give him for food. I missed him. He was so proud of me now that I was at university. My Father died when I was in second year at university—a day before my birthday. It was very strange to have lost my parents in the month of August, separated only by a few years. Father had been so lonely after Mother's death. He seemed to need Mother in a very basic, but important way. After his death, each of us at home was suffering so much from the death of my Mother and then my Father.

In the end of the fourth year of university, people who knew me came up before the results were announced and said they knew I would get high marks. I did graduate with a second upper class in my Bachelor of Commerce degree—the highest standing a student could achieve in that option.

In three months I had my first job as an internal auditor for Graffin College. When I moved on to be an Accountant at Standard Charter

Bank, Mumias Sugar Company also gave me an offer on their management trainee programme. I fast tracked my way through a two year Management Trainee Programme at Mumias in one year. By 2001, I had the position of the Head of the Outgrowers Accounts at Mumias Sugar Company. I maintained the books for 65,000 farmers. Now I am the Tax Manager, or what is called, the Systems and Compliance Accountant."

Whycliffe lifts his glass and takes a deep breath.

"I am married and a father of a baby, named Marie-Sandra. My wife had to drop out of her Medical Assistants' course when she had the baby, but I am hoping that she can get into a college closer to where we live so that she can finish her course. I am clearing my examinations for the British Accountancy Chartered Institute of Management Accountant of England and Wales (CIMA). At present, I am beginning my Masters degree by correspondence.

My younger sister works in the canteen that I set up near the Mumias Estate School. She has truly changed her life. My Aunt and Uncle, whom I used to live with in Nairobi, are now living near me and I am supporting them. My Uncle is sickly now and I help pay for his medicines and doctor. I assist some of my other Aunties too. My nephew is very ill in hospital, close to dying. His Father is also ill. I wonder if it is that dreadful disease we never are able to talk about here, but is causing the death of millions on our continent.

Everlyne, who stays with us, is not a relative, but a poor young woman. She was introduced to me by the old lady who gave money to me as a child. Because this old woman helped me when I was young, I wanted to assist a person that she could not support—although she would have if she had enough resources. Now Everlyne works in the Canteen and helps around our home. I am hoping we can get her into some training or college.

In my old primary school I provide money for awards and counselling and I am hoping to open a library for the school, with the help of one of the former A.C.C.E.S. Agents. Sometimes, I think helping all these people stretches my resources very thin. But I earn more money than all of them put together so I have a duty to assist them. My life is full of people who need me so I don't have as much time for my role of Chairperson of the graduates' alumni's Finance Committee at A.C.C.E.S. I am most proud we have been able to set up the A.C.C.E.S.—C.A.A.A. Savings and Loans Program. Providing loans and training the graduates to set up small businesses is a productive way to encourage these young men and women, A.C.C.E.S. and CHES graduates, while they wait for a turn in the economy as jobs become available. I like to give back to others since I have received so much myself."

Whycliffe stops talking. He appears as if the walk in the past has taken a great deal of energy from him. I ask him what he has learned from all that has happened in his life.

"I have learned so much. The first is aggressiveness. Maybe you would call it assertiveness. My Mother told me the best way to have success is to be aggressive. When you meet anyone, you should try to get money to help you make your way in school and life. You know that a lady in the United States has given me study materials for GMAT, which is the exam required for graduate school in the United States.

Another important thing is being honest. In my job I am known for my honesty. It has assisted me to go all through the levels of banking and business. In fact, Mr. Chigala used to leave me in his house to look after it until he returned from a trip.

Also, I will never forget my humble and simple background, my beginnings. I am a very earthy man, but I know that I can do anything I put my mind to. I see myself in my mind as the boy I once was. The boy who never washed his feet when Chigala took him to go to the market is branded on my brain. No matter how wealthy I become, I will never lose my roots. I will have to love all my relatives in order to succeed. I will never develop a revenge mission. I have to see people around me succeeding. It is only poverty that caused the hatred between my Father and his stepbrothers.

Finally, I have also learned the power of a role model. From the advice of the A.C.C.E.S. Agents, with their education and experience, I feel I have a lot farther to go in to my education. I want to get a Masters and PHD. The people at A.C.C.E.S. have challenged me and I have to challenge others. I think that is the most important thing I have learned from all that has happened to me."

Whycliffe stops. A smile fills his face. And the room.

Whycliffe Kibusu

A man of success, driven to help others,

Aware of his turbulent beginnings and the love of his Mother,

Always moving aggressively towards success.

Of the earth, never forgetting his roots.

Hard-working, compassionate and forgiving,

High powered Accountant and Taxation Manager.

◙ *Elisha Ongoya*

"This conversation is exactly the kind of talk I love. So many people don't take the time to listen to the stories of other people's lives," Elisha exclaimed when we met. "I am so excited that you are writing the life stories of some of our ACCES graduates. That Canadian organization has made such a difference in so many of our lives in Kakamega, Kenya. In fact, I think the graduates number around six hundred."

Elisha was a delight to meet. At exactly the time we had agreed upon, a young man in a navy-blue suit and white shirt, with a blue striped tie, dashed across the Fairview Hotel lobby in Nairobi, and strongly shook my hand, which included a grasping of the thumb—a custom common among the Luyha people of Western Province. He started talking immediately, with a flowing rush of words, as articulate in person as he was in his emails.

"It is so good to meet you. I enjoyed reading your messages from Kakamega. I have been so busy completing my law degree, coaching our team that is going to the All-Africa Human Rights Moot Court competition in Younde, Cameroon, and getting my legal attachment for next year. That's the intern lawyer's placement we locally refer to as our *pupillage* in a law firm. I am going to graduate with distinction from the Bachelor of Law programme at the University of Nairobi this summer."

This urbane, outgoing man and I took our seats in the reading lounge at a table near a floor-to-ceiling window, allowing us to see the strong mid-day sun dappling on the large leaves of a facia tree covered with scarlet bougainvillea.

"First of all, you have to know this. My hero, my role model, while I was at law school, was Nelson Mandela," Elisha exclaimed instantly. "He played such a crucial role in conflict resolution in South Africa. In his book, *Long Walk to Freedom,* Mandela said that it was the lack of opportunity and not the lack of ability that has hindered his people. And also Martin Luther King Junior was another hero for me because he had a similar message."

Elisha referred to his tribal background when he made that reference to Mandela. The Luyha tribe was known for being the poorest and most uneducated people in Kenya, with little opportunity for work.

His cell phone rang. His responses to the person on the telephone indicated the nature of the call.

"You have to appear at the Kilimani Police Station to give a statement."

"No. I will be with you. I will take a Night Bus to Kakamega."

"Then the case will be held in the Vihiga Law Courts."

"I'm promising you that we will win the whole thing."

He finished in his upbeat fashion, and slipped his cell phone back into his jacket pocket. He turned back to his story.

"I try to follow Professor Nabutere's challenge to think globally and act locally. To do that, I must understand the needs of the local people. I just can't sit in an office in Nairobi. There are so many human rights issues in Kenya. As a lawyer I must assist those people. I also challenge my colleagues to do the same. Every year I spend one to two weeks with my local people, the Luyha, so that I never forget what my past was like and what I need to do for my people. And, on the other hand, during my time at the University, I felt that I must lead my university across the globe, firstly in Moot Court competitions and, secondly, in whatever other opportunity that the future holds for me. I learned long ago I must never squander any opportunities."

It took only a brief hint to start Elisha back on his beginnings.

"I was born in 1979 in Emuhaya, a Division of Vihiga District, in a poor and down-trodden background. My family had a quarter of an acre of land where they still live. Since my childhood, we raised vegetables and few other crops. My Father was part of the subordinate staff in the Ministry of Agriculture. This is the general term for lower cadre staff, including cleaners, storekeepers, and junior clerical staff. I was the fourth-born child out of seven. Three cousins of an even poorer background lived with my family after I finished my secondary education. The sparse morsels we had were shared with them. It was an enormous load for my parents, but they had little choice because two of my cousins had experienced the death of both parents. In our culture, it is the custom to take in your brother's or sister's children if something happens to their parents. It did mean, though, that there were ten children to feed and clothe and send to school.

My Mother was a housewife and the gardener of our family. She grew potatoes and cassava—both foods that filled our stomachs against an aching hollowness. Eventually, as I got older, our living conditions seemed to stabilize. With the measly resources Dad had struggled to amass, we acquired a grass-thatched, three-roomed *banda*, a hut, with a one separate room as a kitchen. Eventually a store-room and some animals were added. We children slept in one room. It was a lifestyle we were born into so, in my childhood, it seemed normal. With the benefit of hindsight and having interacted with a cross-section of humanity during my days as a university student, I have come to the conclusion that it was a sub-human life in all its manifestations.

My Dad paid my fees for Esirabe Primary School. When I joined Standard One, which is the same as the first year of your elementary school, in January 1986, the government purchased the books and pencils that students needed. I remember we did our assignments in notebooks that had been cut in half.

Later on, there was a change in government policy. What came to be known as cost-sharing was introduced, whereby the parents had to share the cost of education. At this point, the government stopped making available the books and other writing materials for the pupils. The burden had to be born by the parents. This is when I began writing on separate pieces of paper that I brought from home. I would bring them back home after I had a number of sheets for each subject and Dad would take them to his work to staple them together. When I had a certain number of those self-made notebooks, I counted that I had enough books for each curriculum.

Dad paid the other fees needed for me to attend primary school in Kenya. Although I cannot recall the exact figures, I know the amount was in the tune of 10 Shillings for the watchman's fee and 3 shillings for the report card. In total the amount would be less than 21 cents Canadian for every academic term, but affording this was, surprising as it may sound, not easy.

These myriad of fees that must be paid for a child to go to school prevents so many children in rural Western Province of Kenya from going to school. In total, my Father paid a conservative figure of 500 Shillings (just over $9.00 Canadian) per year for me to attend primary school.

Other than school, there was little else in my childhood to do except reading, looking at the few animals I watched over, and gardening with my Mother. In my rural home, like many other rural homes in Western

Kenya and indeed most rural parts of this country, such luxuries as swimming, watching movies, reading newspapers, and other modest forms of life are a big rumour. No child grows up knowing what these activities are. We only get to stumble upon them very late in our lives when we start to interact with others in the city during our academic pursuits.

I first saw a television set when I was thirteen years of age. I never saw a video player machine until I was a second year, Form Two, student in high school and I first used a computer at university. This is the reality in many parts of the Third World and my Abanyole people, who are part of the Luyha tribe, are not exempt from this state of misery. The life-style was a blessing in disguise because what I spend most of my time doing bore fruit in later life: particularly reading, thinking and observing carefully.

When it came my time to go to secondary school, we needed to pay 9,000 Shillings ($150.00 Canadian). Father's salary was approximately one eighth of that amount. He still had to feed and support ten children. The challenge of coming up with the fees almost marked the end of my academic life. I truly thought my schooling had come to a finish. It was a severe challenge in which my primary school Head Teacher, Mr. Jeremiah Abwala, took a hand in resolving. I feel highly indebted to him in this regard. He saw my potential early in my life—before I even discovered it. He vowed to help me realize it. He knew the Agent for CHES and he introduced me to her.

When I met that Agent, she described Mr. Abwala, as "Jeremiah the Prophet," because he promised her that I was going to excel in my exams. True to his word, when our primary school's national exam results were announced, I emerged top of my class.

I'd been called for secondary school admission to Nyang'ori Secondary School within the Vihiga district of Western Kenya, but CHES had a policy that they would not sponsor students there. It was another impediment that I had to think my way around. Indeed, the English saying, "misfortunes don't travel singly," found a practical expression in my life. I asked the Agent to write a letter to Kakamega Secondary School to introduce me to the Head Master and, also, to Musingu High School. The letter stated CHES would pay my school fees on condition that I was admitted to either of the schools. I was working under the belief that friends, neighbours, church members, and all my well-wishers would give me money for the other fee—the fifteen percent remaining after CHES paid the eighty-five percent of the total fees requirements.

One of my previous Head Teachers during my early childhood days, who is now a retired inspector of schools, took note and asked for my educational details. He followed-up himself at the Kakamega Secondary School. In addition, a friend of my Father who had been a high school teacher and had taught with the Head Master of Musingu Secondary School, provided a letter of introduction for me. His letter got me an interview and my outstanding achievements in primary school guaranteed me a position in the Musingu School.

This opportunity was the greatest moment in my life. I knew it was a turning point in my life because I was certain that I would do well at high school and this would open the next doors of opportunity. I never had a history of squandering opportunities in my life.

I went back to see the Agent at CHES who wrote a cheque for their part of the school fees. I used the well-wishers' donations to help pay the other fifteen percent, but I had no money to afford the other necessities, like shoes. The first shoes I put on were in Form One. They were old shoes repaired by our village cobbler to fit my feet. My Mother's Aunt gave me a box to carry my few belongings. I had nothing in terms of pocket money so I never went to the canteen for lunch at school. Instead I read in the library. No matter how much I went without certain basic necessities, my Father impressed upon me that I was to do well at school so that I would never embarrass his friend who had played such an instrumental role in introducing me to the Headmaster of Musingu High School.

The CHES policy was that a scholarship student had to be among the top third of the number of students in the class for at least two out of the three academic terms to maintain his/her continued sponsorship. I took that challenge seriously. I spent time on reading and studying. In the evening I would play a few games and then back to my books I went. I developed good working relationships with my teachers so they would see me in a positive light. I found the teachers and many of the students had more refined Kiswahili and English than I spoke. I had been raised in the village where the emphasis was on the local language, rather than English and Kiswahili. I spent hours practicing those two languages in conversations with other students and some teachers. It surprised many that during my second year at the University, I was the seventh best public speaker on the continent at the All-Africa Human Rights Moot Court competition among the English speaking contestants. This directly reflected on how much I had improved in English, which was a foreign language for me during my early high school days.

At Musingu, I met students from well-to-do family backgrounds who had attended primary schools in the urban areas of Kenya. My confidence that I could compete with these students was almost impaired as I compared my background to theirs. But, at the end of the first term, I was in seventh place out of the 210 students. My self-confidence blossomed. From then on, I participated in assemblies, school symposiums and countless clubs, including accounting, history and geography. My leadership and my ability, even then, to talk fluidly made my teachers aware of me. They developed a positive interest in what I was doing. They admired my skills in using novels and other authoritative literature as models for my debates.

I found I was soon appointed the Laboratory Prefect, with unlimited access to the Lab. I used to study there because it was quiet and orderly. In fact, I found I loved the scientific process of thinking with its emphasis on problem-solving. I performed exemplarily in my courses because of all the time I spent studying in that Lab.

I also was a top student in English and Kiswahili at the end of my fourth-year high school course. The spin-off of all my reading in these two subjects was that I developed a life-long interest in African literature.

When I visited the CHES Agent, I impressed her with my results and she began to call herself my "second mother." However, there were no extra funds available. Raising the fifteen percent of the fees, which was approximately 900 Shillings each year, an equivalent of about $15.00 Canadian, was my greatest challenge. I encouraged my Dad to get others to give, as well as the teachers at my secondary school. He had great success. Their donations saw me through school.

I finished Form 4 with straight A's achievement in the Kenya Certificate of Secondary Education (K.C.S.E). It was the first time in the history of the school, since it was established in 1965, that a student had achieved this high grade. Indeed, it was the highest possible grade in the Kenya Certificate of Secondary Education. I was told it was a landmark performance. Before the examinations, we were told by the Head Master that no student had achieved a straight A grade in the history of the school. As I wrote the exams, I set my own challenge to get all A's. What I did, then, was to raise the bar of success for myself. A sense of victory plumped my chest when I realized that I met my goal. When I found out my results, I also was beyond myself with excitement and anticipation because then I knew I would get a place in a university and a Government Bursary from the Higher Education Loans Board (HELB)

Fund. HELB is a government funded loan scheme for poor, but able, students in institutions of higher learning. I applied immediately for the HELB loan because I knew I qualified on a number of accounts. A.C.C.E.S. was my strongest supporter, having provided me with a scholarship for all my years of training. Without that scholarship, I could not have gone through the university.

My second challenge was to decide on an academic focus. My parents wanted me to take medicine because my work as a doctor would help get our family out of poverty. They had encouraged my older sister to go into nursing and she was now a student, on scholarship, at a nursing school. But my childhood in a society where I was part of the downtrodden made me believe I had a calling to take on a career which would help establish a better society, not just improve our family's economic need. My religious upbringing as a child and my secondary school experience had nurtured in me the importance of a person pursuing his own personal goals in life. I choose Law, Commerce and Science Education, in that priority, on my university application forms.

Until this time I had never disagreed with my Dad. But now I was determined to follow the career dictated by my beliefs and goals. I stood my ground with my Dad, even when I appeared to be a recalcitrant boy.

"What will you do after this training?" he kept repeating to me.

"If I was after money, I would be swayed by you," I responded. "I want, most of all, fulfillment in my career. Law is my calling."

Dad wouldn't give up. He even brought me to Nairobi to change my courses into Bachelor of Medicine just before the university academic term started. The Admission office was closed, so we couldn't change the course options on the application forms.

Over the two years between secondary school and university, my Dad and I talked about my career many times. Finally he agreed to my choice when he saw he couldn't budge me. In truth, when I look back, he actually played an active role in helping me think out my choice of career: why I saw it as important, what my goals were, how I would achieve them, and how would I know that I had achieved them. These were questions I posed to myself so I did not regret I hadn't followed my Father's instructions to change my career choice. During that time I was supported in my choice by the encouragement given by my former secondary school teachers, particularly my high school geography teacher, Mr. Wycliffe Oboka.

At the end of those two years, I was firm and resolute in my decision. I joined the Faculty of Law at the University of Nairobi on the twelfth of October, 1999. My Dad still hoped, in his heart of hearts, that I would change my mind and go into medicine. But I knew the final journey had begun. Although others had paved my way, the challenge ahead was immense.

I focused on my studies. I knew I had to do well because I had a cause to pursue. My only entertainment was reading books from the library and having intellectual discussions with other students.

In the second year a group of students and I organized to participate in a Moot Court session as an extra-curricular activity. This was a hypothetical court situation where the participants, playing the role of counsel or advocates representing imaginary parties, argued a problem that tended to reflect contemporary legal issues before a bench of judges, who were experts in the branch of the law in question.

After the first semester of my second year of study, I performed dismally in the Moot Court competitions because I didn't understand the procedures. Knowing that I could learn through my mistakes, I set out to find out everything about Moot Courts. I kept a quote from Oscar Wilde on my wall: "Experience is the sum total of mistakes that one has made in his lifetime."

By the end of the second year at university I was part of a team sent on the Trans-Africa Moot Court competition to Arusha, in Tanzania. I was feeling very insecure because we were competing against fourth-year law students from other faculties who, in the ordinary nature of things, would be expected to have a better grasp of the legal issues and concepts in dispute. What a surprise it was for me when we won. That achievement gave me my greatest motivation to continue on in Moot Court competitions.

In my third year I went to the All-African Human Rights Moot Court in Cairo, Egypt. My Mother was so worried about me going on the airplane. She couldn't even imagine ever being on a plane. This Moot Court competition attracted high participation and fifty-two Law faculties from all corners of the continent were in attendance. I met many scholars there. At the end of the contest, our team was strong and we won. In addition, I had shaped my mind on what I intended to do for my future studies—International Human Rights Law, particularly, the African aspects of human rights. In November 2002, I attended a free International Humanitarian Law Course in Pretoria, South Africa.

Early in 2002, I applied to the East Africa Moot Court organizers to attend the competition in Arusha, Tanzania. Sadly, I found out that those who had competed before could not re-enter the competition again. To keep involved, I became a trainer. I coached Godfrey Musila and other colleagues and went with them to the competition. My challenge to them was simple.

"We can't lose. Although winning twice is not easy, we can't come this far and lose. We've done it before and we'll do it again. Although we were not necessarily there to beat anybody, we were definitely there to protect ourselves from getting beaten."

We did win again. Later, I represented my faculty at Philip C. Jessup Competition in Washington, D.C., named for an outstanding judge at the International Court of Justice at The Hague. I realized the expectations for me were very high. It was not easy because I knew I was competing with students from Harvard and other universities of that level. Our team was also amazed that we, a group of students from a Third World Country, were going to Washington. Before we could go to the international rounds of the championship, we had to beat a team from Moi University, also in Nairobi. In preparing for the competitions, it was me who took the lead in pushing my colleagues. We were always awake until 2:00 a.m., working like dedicated lawyers-to-be. I understood that, with sufficient energy and fight, we would get through. It was our driving belief that the Moi team may have prepared for competition, but never had they been against a team from the University of Nairobi. We found that they were worthy opponents. However, we won—much to our delight.

Then we began our rigorous preparations to go to the competition of the top sixteen teams in Washington. It was an historic moment because, since 1959, no African team had participated in the penultimate rounds of the top sixteen teams. I stressed that we were not saying we would win, but that we were not giving the others a chance to beat us. A subtle difference, but very important.

I remember, in Washington D.C., during the Moot Court competition we had to wear Maasai costumes to represent the Kenyan cultures. And I am not Maasai! However, we were proud to have such a distinct Kenyan identity as a country. In the competition, we were placed against teams from Turkey, who had beaten us for the last two years, and then with Australia, Macedonia and Turjikistan. I led my faculty's team to eighth position. We lost to India in the third quarter-round. It was no mean achievement.

That performance marked the highlight of my curricular activities. I served as an advisor to those attending the competition in July 2003, especially Godfrey Musila. I truly felt I was following my calling as I led the team.

I finished my law courses, at the undergraduate level, on July 4, 2003, and immediately joined the Kenya National Council for Law Reporting, as an intern. All official law reports in Kenya come from there so my learning continued. I found a law firm, Mohammed & Muigai Advocates, for my statutory attachment-year. It is a leading law firm in Nairobi. I have been gaining untold experience in the litigation of all the areas of law. I have a keen interest in criminal and human rights law and I hope this firm will mould me into an excellent lawyer.

I still plan to complete my Masters degree and then my doctorate in Human Rights Law at overseas universities. I will pursue all avenues to realize my dream of further studies. It will take a steady and determined fight to achieve my dream, but my childhood experiences have taught me good strategies for success. I never despair. I will not abandon my dreams. I have always believed in shaping my destiny. In life there are those who start with a foundation already laid down by their predecessors—either parents or family friends. As for me that was not the case. I know I wanted that support so badly, but it was in a wishful dream for me. I, therefore, have had to re-arrange my strategies so I could keep pace with those people who started out with advantages. It is this re-arrangement of strategies that finds expression in confidence, hard work, determination, persistence, patience and networking that I use to determine my destiny. My yet-to-be born son or daughter should not begin from a life of disadvantages like the one I began from. I feel like a visionary who borders on Utopia. Some people see things that are and ask, "How did it happen?" I prefer to imagine things that have never been, and then ask "Why can't it happen?" I remember in one of Eleanor Roosevelt's speeches she said something like the future lies in those who believe in the beauty of their dreams.

When I was young, it was the next class that I craved to make it to. At the end of Primary School, I knew something had to be done so I could move forward or I just would become a houseboy. But a scholarship intervened! How many others have gone down the drain because there have been no acts of benevolence for them? CHES and later A.C.C.E.S. made life change for me so I could attend school. Something, like that, always came in just at the point when I most needed it.

I have done what I started out to do—become a lawyer. The disappointment I caused my Dad now has changed. I still tell my parents and colleagues I have a moral duty to assist someone else. That is what CHES and A.C.C.E.S. have done to me. I used to be told that those who sponsored CHES and A.C.C.E.S. students were not people of the *creme de la crème*. They were teachers, businesspersons, nurses and other professionals like that. Therefore, I was being told I didn't need to become a tycoon to assist others, just someone like the person who provided my A.C.C.E.S. scholarship. It is important to remember if you give a man a 1,000 Shillings as a loan to go to school, then you will have changed his life with this one act of benevolence.

Elisha Ongoya

Verbose, enthusiastic, driven,

Professional in demeanour and style,

A man passionate about making a difference.

This lawyer, of quick intellect and boundless energy,

Captures attention from the first moment of meeting.

▨ *Connie Ochieng*

*M*y name is Connie Ochieng and I am 24 years old. My childhood as a girl in a small village in Western Kenya was a difficult road to walk to the destination that waited for me in adulthood.

I am a Luo, living in Luyha territory. As a woman in the Kakamega area, I am caught between our Kenyan past and the present way of living, still dominated by men. Today Luo and Luyha men have the legal right to be polygamous. Each man can have as many wives as he can support. The larger his family is, the more status for him and his tribe. Custom also says that all women must be under the protection of men. Therefore, most women marry young.

My beginning was anything but being born into a bed of roses. My family of eight lived in a one-room hut with a thatched roof on a small *shamba*, or farm, where my Grandfather and Uncles also lived in their own huts. All of my family belonged to the fifty percent group of Kenyans who lived below the poverty line. That meant my family existed on less than one dollar a day. All I can remember from way back then is my sister and I lying heaped on some rags in a corner with the rain dripping on us. My three brothers were huddled under an old blanket in another part of the room.

I know we helped my Mother to go daily to the river to bring water back to our home. We worked the land to produce the food; gathered scraps of wood to cook with; and looked after our hut. We prepared the meals, ground the maize and washed the clothes by hand in a container of water. All through this daily work, I realized that I wanted to be different than the women around me, but I knew, even as a little girl, that life could not be hurried.

I was the third-born, having an older brother and sister. Two boys and a girl followed me. I have been told that it was around the time when I was born that things changed in my family. It was then, they said, that my Father was laid-off, or re-trenched as we called it, from the Kenya Railway because of one mistake at his station. There were no benefits when a Railway employee was laid off. A man was expected to fend for himself and for those he supported. Unfortunately, my Father found his fate very humiliating.

It is an understatement to say that our life became almost too difficult for me to bear. Father drank and became more frustrated when he couldn't get another job. There was little food. My Mother raised the vegetables and had to sell many of them to make a little cash for our survival. The main crop she grew was a green leafy vegetable, called *Nderema*. I helped my older brother and sister pick the tough leaves off the stalk of each plant. I was small-boned, but strong. I moved more quickly than my brothers. My Mother took the leaves from us and boiled some of them in a pot. We children drank the vegetable water. She then continued to simmer the mashed leaves with more water so we had, at least, the mossy green liquid to fill our stomachs for another day or more. After the Long Rains were over, the cassavas, maize and beans were ready. Mother divided them up. Some were sold to buy seeds for the next crop; the less perfect produce was used for our food. We had no money for clothes or shoes, medicine or soap.

My life didn't get any better when our family moved to Shikavala, a village consisting of a cluster of small *shambas*, farms, a tiny market square, and a primary school. Our *shamba* was close to the northern part of the Kakamega Rain Forest. The forest was a living remnant of 15,000 years ago. At that time the forest covered 240,000 hectares in Kenya and Uganda. Now it is down to one-tenth of that size. Too many droughts, too many people cutting trees to cook their food and too much commercial exploitation of trees. My Mother can remember in the 1960's when the forest still covered part of Kakamega. As a child, I recall going into the thick rainforest and listening to the forest come alive with birds' songs. Their chittering, yattering and chirping together created a morning symphony. When we climbed the rocky path of a steep hill, we saw the forest at our feet: a canopy of trees in tones of greens with small open areas of grass and the Yall River snaking through the land.

The bickering and screaming between my Mother and Father was constant during those years when my Father was drinking so much. My Uncles did not help us out at all. I can remember one saying, "Look at those poor ones", but never did they bring any food or clothes over to us. Then my Grandmother died. Her death only made more conflict since my Uncles and my Father fought over who would get her section of land on the *shamba*.

I just wanted things to be peaceful. I listened so carefully to what was going on and I asked lots of questions. Even as a very young child, I used to wander over to the nearby Indangalasia Primary School. I loved to hear the children's voices chanting and singing, so full of happiness in their classrooms. I would stand on the edge of the field and watch them laugh and play during their break-times. The students went back into class, and the fields became silent. I felt the screaming inside my head. But it reminded me that things would be better when I, too, went to school.

When I was five years old, in 1985, I went over to the Matende Nursery School at the beginning of the first term, in January. I thought I was the perfect age to start primary classes and I wanted to go into the peacefulness of a classroom so much. I was heartbroken when the teacher told me that I was too young to start school. Tears filled my eyes as I shuffled back out to the playing fields. I was devastated that I would have to wait a whole year before I could enter this place, so different from where I came.

I went many times that year to my Uncle's *banda,* hut, and told him how much I wanted to go to school. Little did I know that my Mother was also talking to my Uncle. He provided my Mother with a piece of the land where she could grow some sugar cane to sell. When the next school year rolled near, my Uncle called me over to tell me how smart he thought I was and how he knew that I wanted so badly to go to school. He bad-mouthed my Father because he drank and did not work to help us out. Then he said something that made my life glow, like the sky does when the red disc of the sun rises in the dark blue sky, seconds after six in the morning. He had decided that I could use his name and that he would pay my school fees. I could go to my beloved school! I was so happy that I danced and sang around his home.

At the school opening, in 1986, when I went to school, no one told me that I had to go home. I remember feeling almost delicious with the sheer delight of being in a classroom where there was quietness and no fighting. I loved to learn. I took off with excitement down this open road of knowledge. I didn't want to leave at the end of the day. My Mother was very supportive of me. She sold the sugar cane from her new crop on the weekends so she could buy the books I needed. I was determined that I wouldn't let her down. I aced all the tests that year.

Because I was so happy at school, I didn't care that my stomach screamed from the claws that never ceased to clench it. I would get up at 6:00 a.m. Another day of hunger dawned. If we did have enough money to buy maize, each of us would get a cupful of red sorghum porridge. If my Mother couldn't buy the sorghum, we drank lots of water. When the potatoes or cassavas were ready, we ate some of them for our breakfast, as well as our supper. I wanted to eat something after my stomach had tormented me most of the day.

At the end of Standard One I was the second highest position in my class. It was the first time that I had read books or held a stubby pencil in my hand to write in my notebook. My teacher showed me how to cover my notebook with a newspaper jacket so it would last the year. I worked hard all day and did my homework during the lunch hour, instead of playing outside with the other children. I had no time after school to complete my assignments because I had to go into the forest with my sister and gather small pieces of wood for our *jiko,* the hearth to cook on. Our *jiko* was very simple: three very old stones in a triangular shape. We put twigs and small bits of branches into it and lit them. Then our Mother put a big clay pot, filled with water and maize, on top of the fire.

All through the primary levels, I led my classes. Every one of my teachers liked me. They talked kindly to me and supported me to the point of buying my books. In 1993, I completed Standard Eight, just the same as Grade Eight in Canada, with a very high 450 marks out of 600 marks on the final examinations. I was so proud of my achievement, but my hopes were soon dashed for another time. My Uncle told me that he couldn't pay the secondary school fees. He had to finish paying the fees for my older brother, but he would pay for me to repeat Standard Eight so that I could remain in school.

While I was repeating my eighth year, my Father developed lung cancer. My Mother was shocked. She couldn't understand his illness. He coughed and wheezed. We couldn't afford any medicines. We all pitied him, even though he was still mean and nasty.

One day, during that year of repeating Standard Eight, Josephine, a lady from Emusala, came up to me outside our classroom at the end of a history lesson. She told me that there was a lady at CHES, in Kakamega, who would help me go to secondary school. CHES would give me a scholarship to pay all my fees, except for fifteen percent. We would have to pay that small amount. I told her that I didn't know where CHES was. She gave me careful directions to CHES House. Josephine told me that I should bring my Mother and Father, and she also gave me enough shillings for all of us to take a *matatu*—one of the local Nissans that nearly all Kenyans use to get from one place to the next. I felt my soul was in tatters and I was so afraid. I was in my second year of Standard

Eight, getting excellent marks, but I feared that the people at CHES would tell me to go away. In my mind I could see myself working in the fields and marrying some man I didn't know. Josephine woke me from my dark, fearful thoughts when she asked me for my school-leaving certificate so that she could drop it into the Agent at CHES before I went there in the next few days.

Two days later, it was time to go to CHES house. Mother had washed our clothes the day before. We all changed and my Father, Mother and I caught a *matatua* near the corner. My sick Father had already been out to the bar drinking that morning, but he brought me a small novel, *Pride and Prejudice,* that he had purchased from a kiosk in the market. I realized then that he must have valued education, though I never heard him say anything in that line. But his gift of a book must have meant that.

The *matatu* bounced along the dirt road in the rain, past the giant trees of the Kakamega Rain Forest. Eventually we reached Kakamega. I was so excited. I hadn't been to this town before. The main highway that ran through the city had still some of the large trees remaining from the long ago time when the Rain Forest covered this area. Along the road were some big buildings with mould covering their painted walls, as faded as the mist on a cold night. There were many small *duchas*—small stands selling second hand clothes, fruits and beans, hardware and baskets.

The *matatu* let us off at the stop in Lurambee, in the east part of Kakamega. We walked past the little kiosks, displaying fruits, vegetables, chicken and beef, and then a hut where a woman waited outside to have her hair cut. Finally we reached the gate with a small sign indicating CHES. Nervously I went ahead of my parents. I worried what I would do if they wouldn't help me. Perhaps they wouldn't believe my story. I had carried my five letters of invitation to attend secondary schools, even one from the prestigious Mukumu Girls.

The Agent greeted me at the office door and asked me to sit down inside. She gave me lots of forms to fill in and asked me to write about my life. She even asked me why I had decided to attend Mukumu Girls Secondary School, since I had letters of invitations from five schools to choose from. I told her that I would leave the decision up to CHES and I would attend wherever they wanted me to. She said I must return with a letter from our Sub-Chief that outlined our financial needs and explained why my Father couldn't pay the school fees. I was so excited that I wanted to rush home to our village and get the letter immediately.

After the Sub-Chief wrote the letter, I took the same trip, this time by myself. Once the Agent looked at the letter, she told me that I had a scholarship to Mukumu Girls Secondary School—as a boarder. A feeling of absolute joy filled my soul, like a bird that has been released from its cage to fly in freedom. For the next four years I would live at this school where girls from very wealthy families also attended. I felt that I was floating three feet above the red linoleum floor. I knew that this was the turning point of my life. I had suffered so much, but, now, with an education, I would leave my miserable life behind. I would never have such a tormented life again. I would make sure of that. Most of my friends, who had graduated from primary school, had not gone on to secondary school. They had been married and now they were stay-at-home mothers. I was ecstatic.

As I rode home in the *matatu*, I mulled over how I would pay the fifteen percent tuition to CHES that we needed to do each year. I talked it over with my Mother when I arrived home. She went to her younger brother's house to discuss whether he could pay that fifteen percent. At first he said he could not because he had children in secondary school and had their fees to pay. My Mother kept on explaining how it was so important for me to be educated. I was very bright; I worked hard; I wanted to change my life. And she wanted me to achieve that change. Eventually he agreed to pay. In return I would stay with him and work for him during the holidays. If I failed at school, then I would have to look for someone else to pay.

The people were different at the Mukumu Girls School from the place where I lived. In my village, the children and women laughed at me for achieving so well. They kept asking me why I bothered to study so hard when I knew I was going to get married in Form One, which is the same as Grade Nine in other countries. I was upset by their teasing and stopped studying. My Mother and Uncle talked to me and reassured me that I was right in being who I was and in striving for a better life. They confirmed my hard-working, persevering and optimistic nature would take me away from this village to better things.

Shortly afterwards, I took another long *matatu* ride to Mukumu Girls School. It was a long ways south-west of Kakamega and a life-time away from my own home town. I had shopped with the CHES money for my uniform, shoes and book supplies. I took these supplies, a container of salt and a toothbrush in a bag. I didn't have enough money left for a bar of soap.

When I arrived at the school, I saw girls in pretty clothes being dropped off by their parents. I just put my shoulders back and my head up. I was here to change my life. During the first weeks, some girls looked at me as if I shouldn't be there, and they certainly didn't want to come into my bedroom. Others showed some sympathy, as if they understood that it was no fault of my own I was poor and came from a small village far away. Two girls offered me a piece of soap after they saw me picking up small pieces that remained in the shower, squeezing them together to make a bar.

What helped me to survive was that I performed well in the academics. I was always in the top third during Form One. I discovered there were many clever girls in my classes so I missed sleep at night to study so that I could get outstanding marks on the tests.

When I went home during my break time I told my parents all about Mukumu Girls School. The next day, before I was to go to my Uncle's place to work for a few days, my Father gave me 20 Shillings to buy some soap. That touched me because he never gave us any money. He usually kept it for his alcohol.

It was during this time my Mother took me out into the bush and taught me how to make *Chang'Aa,* a horrible drink made from maize. She told me she was so desperate for money that she had to make this brew to sell. She needed food and medicine for my Father and books for my younger brothers and sister who were in school. My Mother and I stayed in the bush at night to make *Chang'Aa* and to sell the bottles of alcohol. We had to do it in the bush to keep the activity private, in fear of the police. When my Mother was sick, I looked after both making the alcohol and selling and transporting it at night. This was the only way we could get some tea or a tin of maize every two weeks. I helped Mother do this on my holidays all through secondary school.

During my year in Form Two, in 1996, Father passed away. Although I didn't like the way my Father drank his life away and made our family's life miserable, I felt depressed by his death. I remembered the times when he had given me something and these thoughts made me sadder. I was very worried about my Mother and how she would make out. Because I was in such an emotional state that year, my marks fell. However, I recovered in Form Three and went back up to a standing in the top third of the class. In Form Four, I received a C+, not a high enough mark to go to university.

After finishing at Mukumu, I was worried. I didn't know where to start to make a new life. It was at the CHES workshop for women that I found hope. They were giving small loans to start raising vegetables. I wanted to apply for this money to buy seeds and raise a crop, but I couldn't. My Uncle needed my help. He had given me the fifteen percent each year to pay CHES. I knew I must give my time to work with him to pay him back for his support.

After the secondary school results were posted, CHES contacted me and told me to apply to A.C.C.E.S. for a scholarship to go for higher learning. I worried because so many others had done better than I did in their final secondary examination that I wouldn't stand a chance for a scholarship. However, I went to A.C.C.E.S. and applied for a scholarship. Luckily enough, I got an Admission Letter to go to Kagumo Teachers College. I specialized in English and German, a language I had become proficient in at secondary school.

The College was in Nyeri, in the Aberdare Mountains—a long way from my home. I needed six hundred shillings for my fare home. To meet this financial challenge, I decided I needed to earn some money while I went to Teachers' College. I got a job fetching water at 30 Shillings (about 50 cents Canadian) a day. Also I weeded at a sugar cane plantation. I saved my earnings for transport and personal needs. My Uncle continued to sponsor me, although he had two of his own children in secondary school. He knew I was a good performer at school and always obedient and humble. I did everything so well that he continued to give me a hand right to the end of my teachers' training.

I graduated in November 2002, with the knowledge it wasn't easy to get a teaching position. However, luck and connections helped me out. My Uncle who had sponsored me knew a friend in the educational field. He asked his friend to talk to a Head Master. This Head Master, of a private school in Kakamega, called me in for an interview. I was hired to teach English and German from January to April 2003. Because it was so far from my home village, I had to rent a two-roomed house, with a bedroom and a sitting room. I bought some food because my Mother couldn't give me any supplies as she was old and could no longer work in the fields to produce her crops. Instead she needed our assistance.

My family said now that I had a job, I had enough money to live on. The problem was that I taught two months without receiving any pay. Finally, the school gave me half of what was owed. Things were really getting tough because I didn't have enough to pay the rent and buy food. I realized then that my life depended solely on me. One night the landlord came and pounded on my door. He wanted his rent immediately. He refused to accept my explanation the school wasn't paying me my salary. I didn't know what to do. Early that morning, as I rolled and tossed on my blanket, I realized I had to ask for help. I had been active in CHES activities since secondary school. I talked to a few of the students' teachers and asked them to assist me. They gave me some money so I was able to toss away my temptation to run back home to my relatives. I was saved from admitting I couldn't manage on my own.

In April 2003, I found an English teaching post at Shikunga Secondary School to help with a month of tutorial classes for a teacher on a leave of absence. Shikunga was one of the secondary schools that CHES had funded girls to attend. I developed a good relationship with the students. The Head Master liked my manner with the students and my commitment to the job. In the school opening in May, the Head Master called me to come in. The Government had the school's vacancies posted in the Shikunga School and in the District. He asked me to make an application. However, I didn't get a chance for an interview because he had to select a teacher from the many graduates who had been without employment for a longer time than I had. The Government said that teachers who had graduated before 1998 had to be hired first. I am still looking for a government teaching position. Right now, I have the job at Shikunga and I'm paid by the Board of Governors.

Although life is not settled yet, I feel successful. I have my secondary school education and teacher training. I am a ready-made teacher and I love my job. I speak German, Kiswihili, English, Luo and Luyha languages. With my knowledge of languages I have a great teaching specialty. I want to make sure no child fails any of my courses. I am so proud to be a teacher because I believe all the knowledge in the world comes from a teacher.

Also, I lead CHES workshops for girls because good female students will bring a changed future for women in Kenya. I will support girls' education. When you educate a woman, you educate a whole village and change a society for the better. I will help other poor women, like me, to get something in their life.

I am determined to improve my own life standards. I will do it! I know that now. Above all, no one should give up in life as it always is a matter of time and one's own efforts that determines the future. I know my future is my own making. CHES and A.C.C.E.S. have opened the doors to this new horizon for me. For that I am so thankful.

Connie Ochieng

A young woman who sparkles with intelligence and creativity.

Articulate and passionate,

Zealous to teach and determined to touch other women's lives.

Hard work has been the benchmark of her success.

A teacher committed to making a difference.

PHOTO COURTESY WAYNE CROSSEN

⬚ *Davis Omamo*

*D*avis Omamo is a very popular man in his village. However, the villagers in Bukura, can't expound on why that is, except that they say he is a man to go to when they need help. Davis' popularity is a measure of his deep pride in being able to assist others. He has not abandoned the people of his roots—as some do when they emerge from the grips of poverty.

Only 27 years old, Davis is a slim, sturdy young Luyha. His high, open forehead is fringed by short black hair smoothly combed. His dark eyes are calm and penetrating; his lips rarely break into a smile. Instead, when things amuse him, his whole face radiates with joy. He is always dressed in either a business suit with shirt and tie, or in attractive casual clothes. In the beginning of his life, things were very different.

In 1976, being the first-born in Bukura in the Western Province was a major event for his parents, but not an auspicious beginning for Davis. Quickly, in rapid succession, the family grew to include five sisters and three brothers. His Mother and Father and their nine children, which became eight after one child died, lived in a *banda*, a circular mud house with a grass thatched roof, on a half acre farm, or *shamba*. Crops were their only source of food and, with the sale of some of their vegetables, the family's income was less than 100 Shillings a week (about $2.00 Canadian).

Bukura was a small, densely populated, rural community. Villagers gathered every day at a stream that ran through Bukura to draw water for their own domestic use. Roads in this area were made of murram—the dark red dirt packed down hard. During rainy seasons they were terribly muddy, while in dry seasons dust was a constant companion.

Davis described his family as a traditional peasant family. His Mother, as the housewife, cared for the land, raised the crops, gathered the wood for cooking and walked to get water. She cooked, cleaned and raised the children. His Father's role was to take a crop, such as cabbage, surplus to the family's needs, and sell it at the market.

When his Father had produce to sell, he would get up early, have hot milk tea and then walk to the market with the cabbages in an old sugar sack on his shoulders. There he would lay the produce on the ground by the *duchas*, the small shops, and stand patiently, chatting to other men, all day until everything was sold or until the day was close to dark. Evening falls early on the equator—around 6:30 p.m. Like all Kenyans, he was determined to get home before the dangers of the darkness emerged. Unknown faces of armed robbers filled every soul with fear.

His Father hurried back from the market to their *shamba* for dinner. When he arrived, hopefully with an empty sack and some coins in his pocket, he would be fed first. After their Father had finished, the children and their Mother would gather to eat in the small sitting room that served as a kitchen, dining room and bedroom. Their portions of *ugali*, ground maize cooked in water and beaten into a paste, accompanied by *sukuma wiki*, a bitter kale-like vegetable, filled the empty cavities of their stomachs. Each person used their first two fingers and thumb to pinch and roll a bite-size piece of *ugali* into a ball which they would then encircle a sliver of the cooked green vegetable. With hunger satisfied, the family prepared to go to bed in the dark *banda*, unlit by electricity, lantern or candle.

Beside the sitting room were two small bedrooms, one for his parents and the other for the four brothers. The four boys, over the years of growing up, went into their tiny room each night. Davis watched over his younger brothers as each laid a sugar sack, gathered from the Mumias Sugar Company, on the smeared dirt floor. Smearing is a regular application of fresh cow dung to the floor to prevent unsavoury creatures, like jiggers, from entering their vulnerable skin from the dirt during the night. Davis shared one old blanket with his brother, while the other two boys slept huddled underneath another one. These two blankets were both purchased from a second-hand stall at the market after his Father had sold some of their cabbages. Never, over the years of their childhood, did they get their own blankets. Their Mother washed those two blankets into thin, tattered cleanliness. The girls, because they were female and therefore of lesser status to their brothers, moved the table in the sitting room to one side, spread old clothes on the floor and slept huddled between layers of rags. Nights were cold, down to about six degrees Centigrade during the months of the Long Rains. It was a special night when the four daughters received their parents' old blanket to cover them. Another sale of vegetables had permitted their Father to buy a new blanket for the matrimonial bed. Later, a small cook hut was constructed outside the main house to store the cooking utensils and to provide a separate space where the mother and her daughters prepared the evening meal. The girls started then to sleep here, along with the poultry.

The days were unendingly the same. Waken in the early morning light, fold up and store the bedding, wash in a bowl of cold water. There was never enough ground maize for breakfast porridge so the children went outside to do their chores and play under the elegant flame trees with only a cup of milk tea in their stomachs. Milk tea is made by throwing a pinch of tea leaves into a pan with hot milk and simmering it for a few minutes. At lunch, except during the hungry months of the Long Rains, they each sipped eagerly a bowl of thin gruel of maize porridge that would still the pangs raging in their stomachs.

Davis eagerly waited for the day he could go the Eshiandukusi Primary School, sitting like a magnet only 500 meters from his home. Going to school meant his parents would have to pay school fees each term. Money from the sale of cabbages and extra *sukuma* was enough only to pay for salt, sugar and, occasionally, clothes or a treasured blanket to sleep under. Paying school fees was a dream, not possible for peasant farmers' children.

His desire to go to school burned so intensely that six-year old Davis walked over to the primary school when it opened for the first term. He was immediately sent home because he did not bring any money for the required fee. That night he devised a strategy: at 10:00 a.m., an hour after class started, he would sneak into the Standard One classroom.

The next day he put on his clean pants and shirt, washed his face and combed his hair. At 10:00 a.m., he slipped quietly into class. Until the teacher noticed his face among the many, Davis learned fascinating things, such as letters and numbers. When the teacher became aware of his quiet presence, Davis was sent home. He waited a couple of days and then went into his class—again after ten in the morning. Finally, the teacher, amazed at his eagerness to learn and his persistence to come to class, invited him to stay. She persuaded the Head Master to permit him to attend school until the fees were paid. Only in Standard Eight, equivalent to Grade Eight in Canada, was the Kenyan government's compassionate grant awarded to him to pay for his school fees and a lunch programme, feeding him milk and porridge every noon. Finally, after seven years, he became a legitimate student, not afraid of being forced out at any point because no school fees had been paid by his family.

During his last year at Primary school, Davis exclaimed to his Mother, "I love school. I can answer all the questions the teachers ask and I can speak English."

"I am so happy I have a son who can speak English as well as Luyha and Kiswahili," his Mom crooned, as she smiled at him.

"School is the only place I can be with my friends. I can see them every day. It is the greatest place to be," Davis said, dancing excitedly around his Mother.

In the Kenyan educational system, examinations ruled supreme. If a student failed two examinations, he or she repeated the whole school year. Marks were converted into a standing for each student in the class, school and district. Every year when the school term ended in November, Davis achieved either the top first, second or third position. In the end of Standard Eight, he faced the problem of bringing in the fees for the Kenyan countrywide examinations. The Head Master called him into his office.

"Davis, you know you need to pay the examination fee. However, the teachers in our school have volunteered to pay your fee. They believe that you will do so well on all your exams you will raise the school's average mark. What an honor for you, and what a privilege for us. Do your very best and study hard. We count on you."

Davis proved that his teachers were right. He was the top student in the country-wide examinations. He led the marks of all the students, raised the school's prestige, and qualified for secondary school. No mean feat for a young man who couldn't study in the evening. The Kenyan Department of Education directed, or "called," him to go to a provincial public secondary school, but his family couldn't raise the money for these fees, which were even larger than for primary school. His Uncle, who was a tailor, had a solution for Davis and his Father.

"Let Davis come to my kiosk and sit close to me to learn how to tailor," his Uncle offered. "He can observe and learn from me. He is bright and picks up things quickly."

"What good would that do him—to learn to sew?" his Father challenged.

"When he has picked up enough, he can go outside my kiosk and sit. People will come along and ask him to do sewing jobs. Then he can bring the money home to help the family."

However, a young teacher came into their world and changed the course of events. Head Teacher, Joshua Chitaha, had just arrived, in 1991, at Imbale Secondary School, located on the brow of a hill looking over a lush valley of small farms and palm trees. He was searching for bright students with excellent marks to come to Imbale to improve their school's standards on provincial tests. He came to talk to Davis' Father. After the ritual of greetings, he stated his reason for being there.

"Mr Omamo, I need some bright students for Imbale School. I know Davis has done very well on his final examinations in primary school. If Davis joins Imbale, I will allow him to enroll free—no fees—for the first term. If he qualifies by getting excellent marks, then I will recommend him for sponsorship by CHES."

"That sounds like an answer to our problem," exclaimed his Father. "Davis doesn't want to be just a tailor."

Davis joined Imbale Secondary School and at the end of the term he was the top achieving student, out of the seventy-four students in Form One, equivalent to Grade Nine in Canada.

He was sent to an interview and readily selected. Four years at secondary school would now be almost free. Davis negotiated with the Agent that he would not pay the required fifteen percent annually. She could keep track of the amount for the four years and Davis promised he would clear the loan when he got a job. Paraffin would also be provided by CHES so that there would be light to study and do homework in the dark evenings. Davis shared that light with his family so his brothers and sisters could also do their studies.

The refrain, "Life is changing," ran through Davis' mind as he studied each night. The fact he would graduate from secondary school opened vistas to him, unimaginable to his Father. All through his four years at Imbale, he maintained his standing as one of the top four students. Food and clothes were not important. Davis revelled in learning, like a young springbok fighting his way to the top position of the herd on the Serengti Plains.

"I felt more at home at school than in my own family's house," he recently reminisced. "The teachers were so supportive and gave me so much encouragement. They kept reminding us to work hard so then we would be successful. Often they said that we didn't know our future, but our determination and strong efforts would take us to the point where we wanted to be when we were older. I loved school. As a CHES student I was given free books to read, lunch, tea, Saturday tuition, extra-curricular activities and paraffin."

From that whirlwind of effort, Davis graduated third in his class with a B Plain (74%) in 1994. He missed a second class of B plus by one mark. His illiterate parents were bursting with pride at Davis' accomplishments.

In Kenya there is a two year gap period from when a student finishes secondary school and begins post-secondary training. During this time, Davis was given a section of his Father's half acre to dig and plant *sukuma* for himself. By December of the next year he had something to sell at the market until February.

Good fortune still beamed on this hard-working young man. The Head teacher, Joram Shiandu, of Ebuchinga Secondary School, located on the road between Kakamega and Mumias, needed a teacher of English. He talked to Joshua Chitaha, still the Head of Imbali School. Joshua highly recommended Davis for that position. Immediately, he had an English teaching job substituting for other subject teachers during their absences. He was paid 1,500 Shillings ($30.00 Canadian) a month during 1995-96.

Ever-focused and self-disciplined, he saved for university. In 1997, he was placed by the Department of Education at Maseno University, a small university, in Kisumu—a city on the north-east side of Lake Victoria. He was given a HELB loan of 40,000 Shillings from the Kenyan government for each of the four university years. His boarding fees at the school residence, food, books and materials were supported also by an A.C.C.E.S. scholarship. Raised in poverty, but with an intellectual brilliance demonstrated during his school years, Davis became one more student A.C.C.E.S. assisted to go to university.

Davis lived a very simple life at university. He ate a small amount of *ugali* and lived frugally to save his money. He realized he had to be very good at managing and saving money because he needed his loan money to assist his younger brother and sisters at school. With Davis' support, his next-in-line brother completed secondary school and went into carpentry training. His sister completed secondary grades without getting good marks and so moved into the tailoring job that Davis had never taken. The rest of his siblings attended primary schools. In addition to financing the education of his seven brothers and sisters, he constructed his own iron-roof circular house on his Father's property. It is the custom of the Luyha tribe when a son becomes an adult, he must have his own separate quarters.

University years were a time for Davis to blossom. He continued to study hard and basked in his belief life was good to him. Only later did he see that he made life what it was.

49

One day, Professor Luvai, his lecturer of Literature, and now Deputy Vice Chancellor at Maseno University, called him into his office. Davis hesitantly slipped through the open door to the book-lined office.

"Davis, I want to meet the student who scored only one mark short of a perfect hundred percent on my Literature exam!" Luvai exclaimed. "Did you go to secondary school in Nairobi?"

"No, I went to Imbale, a school outside of Kakamega. It is a small school, only recently started and funded by Festus Litiku. Festus' Father had funded the Imbale Primary School. He challenged Festus, whose financial successes had been rising, to start a secondary school."

"What a diamond has emerged from that new, rural school. You are brilliant, young man. You will do well in life."

"Thank you," Davis murmured.

"No, I thank you. If you have any problems at university, you just come and see me," Professor Luvai pronounced slowly and emphatically. "I will help you."

Academics, however, did not claim all Davis' time. He entered some major extra-curricular activities that defined his future.

The first project he launched was a Boy Scouts Club called Rangers and Rovers. Never having had the opportunity to be part of Boy Scouts in secondary school, he jumped into scouting activities at Maseno University. He nudged the club into community work, with a first project of organizing a town clean-up of Kisumu.

Kisumu was a busy port town since the early 1900's, but had the feel of a small town, with faded buildings. Sidewalks bustled with pedestrians and hawkers. Warm winds from Lake Victoria swirled old papers and food wrappings along the edge of the streets. Just north-east of the main street, Oginga Odinga Road, was Kibuye Market, an immense, outdoor collection of people selling food, fish, second-hand clothes and furniture.

The University loaned the students in the Rangers and Rovers Club a school bus to take them down to Oginga Odinga Road. Over the morning, they picked up litter from the streets, sidewalks and drains. Then Davis and the other students gathered a crowd around them in front of a large bank and spoke about how to maintain a clean and healthy town environment. The group cheered and clapped their accomplishment.

Later, he became passionate about drama and joined the Drama Club that acted scenes from the "Set" books, texts that were recommended by the Kenyan Department of Education for students at university to study in preparation to answer examination questions. The theater troupe believed viewing these plays would help improve students' understanding and memory of them.

After a while this troupe's play-acting took on a political stance. The actors moved their presentations out to the countryside and performed beside the red dirt roads tracing the routes from one village to the next. They acted political scenes about events taking place in Kenya. Their purpose was to ridicule the political system of the day. Mainly university lecturers and students came into the rural settings to enjoy the satires. Through their laughter, individuals came to understand what they didn't want to happen any longer in Kenya.

Other skits with scenarios about the university took on a moral tone. During the 1990's, students at universities, including Maseno, demonstrated and rioted against the government. The Drama Club's morality plays turned a corner. They stressed that students needed to decide whether demonstrations were the right path to follow. The business community had become loath to employ persons from Maseno University because students were always demonstrating when they didn't like something. The businessmen in the area were afraid they would continue that type of behaviour on the job.

After AIDS was recognized as an official disease by the Kenyan government in 1998, Davis wrote plays that zeroed in on the role of men's promiscuity in spreading HIV. He also wrote an article on the incidence and consequences of HIV in his own village of Bukhuru. The play was featured at the Annual General Meeting of the A.C.C.E.S. Student Alumni in 2001 and is still presented in the villages.

If studies and these extra-curricular activities didn't keep him busy enough, Davis saw another opportunity when he read an advertisement in the newspaper during his fourth year at Maseno. The position was for a one-month enumerator for an N.G.O., Africa Now. He applied and got the job. In that month he was to research the water tanks in the Rift Valley, near Nyanza. Given a driver and a van, he interviewed people and helped them to fill in questionnaires. In the evening he worked up a daily report and worked on a summary report. When he finished the job, Africa Now said they would employ him when he finished university.

But Davis had other plans. He left college, feeling rich. He had enough money to support himself as he finished university in August. When he arrived home in September, a letter was waiting for him at his

Father's homes. In it was an offer for a teaching job at Eshisiru Catholic Secondary School, in Kakamega. The position of teaching English and Literature would pay 4500 Shillings per month, about $75.00 Canadian.

"I can't believe this! I have just graduated," he told his Father. "Other people I know who graduated in Education two years ago don't have a job yet."

"You must be doing the right things, my eldest son," his Mother joined in.

In the two terms he worked at Eshisiru, his students achieved good marks on the examinations which was considered an excellent measure of teacher success. In the third term, he took over the drama program at the school without being paid. He had the young men and women perform the play on HIV he had written and acted at university. In the Nairobi competition, Eshisiru School represented Western Province. They won first place, bringing great honour to their school and their teacher.

Still the doors kept opening. Davis' hard work and talent built a reputation solidly based on his accomplishments. When he officially graduated from Maseno University in March, 2001, he went back to Eshisiru Secondary School. But now he knew he was in charge and life was going to be very different for him.

Ever watchful for new opportunities, he read an advertisement in The Nation newspaper that the Kenya government needed sixty-six teachers of English for the entire Kakamega District. He applied. It wasn't long before word leaked out that the people who applied were teachers who had graduated before 2000. Davis was the only applicant who had graduated in 2000. His transcripts and experiences were so impressive that he was hired immediately to teach English as a government teacher, starting in May, at Lirembe Secondary School. At the same time, he was offered an English position at a private school, Lirembe Girls Academy, very near the secondary school. He took both jobs because, in Kenya, the reality was that it took three months to receive the first salary payment from the public school system, while the private schools paid immediately. It worked out he taught English at the Academy during the day and scurried to the secondary school, which was close by, to present similar classes in the evening until 8:00 p.m. The Lirembe Principal, Joram Shiundu, became his mentor and let him board with his family. On the weekends Davis photographed students in the two schools and bounded into town to get them developed so he could sell them right away to the students.

It took until the third term before he received his pay cheque from the government. He looked for someone to take his position at the Lirembe Secondary School, while he continued to teach at the Girls Academy. He honed his skills and wrote, on his own initiative, a collection of five categories of plays to teach English and Literature. He continued to write plays, one on free primary education. Again he took his all-girls student drama class to the provincial and national levels. Quickly, he became the Head teacher of Languages. When the Principal offered him the position of Deputy Principal, he refused, saying he would do it the following year.

In his classroom Davis shared with his students the personal qualities that had brought him success.

"In primary school, I told the Head Teacher that I had been sneaking and dodging to get into class because I wanted to go to school beyond anything else. I never feared failing ever in my whole life. I like to attempt any challenge. When I hear of a position, I try out for it because I want to go places. To be successful, you have to be persistent. Don't ever give up. If you can follow this advice, you, too, will be to reach your dreams."

After one of these classes where he had shared his beliefs with the students, a girl, called Eileen, stayed behind.

"Mr Omamo, I have heard that you have volunteered to give money to other girls to help them out when they didn't have enough for fees for examinations or extra-curricular things, like drama," she started quietly. "My family has no money and I have to pay my fees or I will be forced out of school. Can you assist me?"

"Because I know you are very bright and you want to be in school, here's what I can do for you, Eileen. I will contact CHES and beg them to assist you. One of my greatest achievements is to help people like you."

Eileen was given a scholarship by CHES and proceeded to do so well in school that she is now the top student of Form Two, equivalent to Grade Ten.

After the first year of teaching Davis had enough earnings to shift to his own rental house in Khayega. It had water and electricity, and even an inside toilet. He bought a very expensive sofa set and his own big, comfortable bed. One day Davis looked at his house and, suddenly, realized that everything in his home was so different from where he had started. A mud hut with no water, electricity, plumbing, bed or sofa.

When his Father visited he was always impressed.

"Davis, are you sure this is your house?" Father asked him every time. "I can't believe you sleep in that thing called a bed. How can you sleep in it?"

"This is truly my house and I enjoy every night's sleep in the bed," replied Davis.

"Well, people think you are very rich," his Father preened. "They talk in the village about how successful you have become. And I appreciate what you give your own family. It would be so difficult to manage if you did not give us the fertilizer, seeds, and food. Without you paying the school fees at the end of each month, your brothers and sisters would not be going to school."

"I know, Dad. I do it because I have the money and I want to help my family. But beyond our family, so many persons come to me and ask for a loan. Even our relatives. They want me to assist them with their children's school fees. They even want their children to come to the school where I teach because they think there will be no fees for them. I can't do that for them. I only give money for seeds because so often the money goes on alcohol. I don't want my family and relatives to be over-dependent on me. I will help when I can, but they must work hard too."

"Son, I will talk to our relatives so they don't bother you so much. I appreciate what you do for us. You are the reason we survive."

"But you know, Dad, I must give the credit to CHES and A.C.C.E.S. for my success and my ability to help you. Without their help, I wouldn't be where I am now. I am different from what I used to me. I do all kinds of things I couldn't have—unless I was a university graduate."

"Davis, you were always so smart and hard-working. You could think up ways to make things happen. I am so proud you are my son."

"But I am not stopping at where I am now. I want to get my Masters in Counselling Psychology. Most of the students who are not performing well in my classes have problems at home. The training in a Masters programme would help me to work with those kinds of people."

"Why do you want to get more education? You are a successful teacher now."

"I have a great desire that my students achieve what I have. That means I try to understand them—and what is preventing them from reaching their goals. But, Father, at present, I am involved in a community development project in Lurambi. I must go and meet with some people about it. See you next week."

Davis was referring to the Lurambi Clean Water Project for which he had received a large grant of money. The project was to organize a group to protect the water springs of Lurambi so that residents would have access to clean water. With a friend, J. Kenyatta, he had written a proposal for funding of $45,000.00 U.S. to the Japanese Embassy and it was accepted. He registered their group and determined how many springs had to be protected, sent off letters to various Ministries in the government to get their recommendations on how to train the citizens of Lurambi, and hired field officers. By September 2003, they started cementing the springs and installing taps on them. Then the people had a clean, running source of water for drinking, cooking and bathing. An important part of the three year project was the workshops that were conducted for the people. The workshops focused on using safe water, achieving good sanitation standards by always washing hands after use of the latrine, building pit latrines in appropriate locations, cleaning indoor and outdoor living areas or compounds, and proper storage of clean kitchen utensils.

This major project was only one of three undertaken by this fast-tracked twenty-seven year old man. Davis was also the Chairperson of the Executive that year for the student alumni of the A.C.C.E.S. graduates, whose goal was to assist others, having been assisted by Canadian donors through A.C.C.E.S.

Now that his life had a fresh, prosperous foundation, Davis took a wife. Rose was literate, employed, and also strove to assist others. She was a Luyha woman and a nurse at Mukumu Mission Hospital, just outside of Kakamega. On November 29, 2003, he married Rose, a woman who fitted his vision of perfect partner. She joined her new husband in the very pleasant home he had prepared on the hospital grounds.

This man has an even bigger dream for the future. He plans to try to run for Member of Parliament in the next election in 2007. Davis is a man whose life was changed by Canadian scholarships. Being helped to be educated, he now assists his own society. Even the local people say he is there to help them. The circle of giving continues. Davis is a Kenyan with a future mapped out.

Davis Omamo

A man with a plan, committed and daring.

Passionate about modern-day causes and issues.

A man whose writing contributes a new look at social issues, like AIDS.

A teacher committed to Kenya's future and change.

A man of action.

Davis in the doorway of his home

Typical grass thatched hut, called a banda

⊠ *Everlyne Musalia*

*E*verlyne sits in the plastic-covered back seat of a taxi, with rivulets of sweat streaming down her face. It is over 30 degrees Centigrade and the humidity is unbelievable. At least now she has arrived at the A.C.C.E.S. compound in Kakamega. The rusty taxi with the sticker, *Jesus Loves Me,* plastered across the back window, stops in front of a high black gate. Jeremiah, the taxi driver, toots the car horn.

"Good thing we're here," Jeremiah smiles as he turns around.

A tall, handsome *askari,* watchman, opens the black metal double gates, and the taxi drives through. The car moves slowly along a rutted gravel pathway—edged on one side by a flower bed, full of greenery and a few yellow and mauve flowers flinging their heads in the puffs of a hot breeze. The taxi makes a sharp turn left and stops in front of a large two-story sandy brick building with a long, open veranda. Large white cans, covered in painted flowers, hold yellow and orange nasturtiums tumbling onto the grass. The watchman runs over to the taxi to welcome Everlyne as Jeremiah pulls the rear door open.

Everlyne, a short, young Kenyan woman, steps out of the taxi and pays Jeremiah. She is dressed in a formal blue business dress—with matching pumps and sparkling rhinestone earrings. Today her hair is styled in a sleek page-boy; tomorrow it will likely be in the tiny braids so popular for the moment in Kakamega. She rushes over to the gated door of the large building housing the A.C.C.E.S. office and apartments.

Quickly Everlyne walks up the stairs into a white plastered reception area which also serves as her office. Four chairs are in front of a half-brick wall. A secretary's desk, two filing cabinets and a narrow table with a chair tucked in are behind the brick divider. Files are scattered over the table.

A young woman waits on one of the chairs while another writes a letter at the table. These are the young Luyhas who have been selected for the A.C.C.E.S. scholarship programme. Everlyne nods at the one woman who looks up from writing a letter to her Canadian sponsor, then she goes over to the other student. She provides information needed about the criteria used for student selection—high achievement at secondary school and a background of poverty.

"It's so good to be back here," Everlyne says to the students.

Light floods through the big screened window. The window has a network of iron bars that shout out concerns about security. In this country, a large building can have an attraction for the gangs of thieves in the Kakamega area. Poverty breeds desperation.

After Everlyne finishes helping the two students, both of them leave. She then strolls into the meeting room where there is an electric stove. A ceiling fan whirls the hot air in fast circles above the wooden table. She takes a thermos filled with milk tea and pours it into a china cup. Each morning, she boils milk with some black tea leaves and adds lots of sugar to make the tea. It is kept it in a thermos for A.C.C.E.S. employees to drink on their breaks.

Everlyne sits at the table under the fan, near the glassless windows. No wisp of air from outside joins the circling hot air above her. She thinks about the young woman she had just interviewed. Lulled by the heat, her thoughts jump back to times past. She decides then to record her story on tape for the book on Kenyans. She also knows that the recording will help her young daughter to know about her Mother's life when she grows up—in case something happens to her before her daughter reaches adulthood. Everlyne has had many bouts of different illnesses, common to the area, and seen so many people die from the disease that is never talked about. She goes over to the shelf and gets the tape recorder. She plugs it in and sits down again, with her tea in hand. She clicks on the record button and begins.

"I was the fourth-born out of six children. Three girls and three boys in our family. My Mother was illiterate. We survived by selling sugar cane and vegetables that we grew on our farm, called a *shamba*. My Father had a second wife in Nairobi. I was about five years old when something important happened. In that year, 1983, my Father ran away from our family to live with his second wife. From then on, we were on our own. Things became very difficult for us.

No matter what had gone on, I was determined to go to school. My Mother was also keen that I should attend school to learn to read and write. She didn't get the chance herself, but she wanted better things for her children. And so, from her efforts, I did go to school. While I progressed through the primary levels, my oldest sister dropped out of secondary school and got married by the time she was eighteen. My next elder sister did exactly the same thing and then my older brother, the first-born son, left school in Standard Eight.

I progressed through primary school and received 61 points on my Kenyan Primary Examinations. I thought that my schooling would end at that point, because my family had no money to pay for secondary school fees. But, one day, my luck turned around because of one simple event. My cousin, who was studying at Ekambuli Secondary School, dropped in to see our family. He left our hut, without taking his school assignments. When my Mother noticed his papers on the chair, she told me to take them to my cousin who would be in class at Ekambuli. By chance, or by God's plan, while I was at the school I saw Ann, the CHES Agent. She approached me and asked me what I was doing at the school. I told her about my errand, explaining that I wanted to attend secondary school. I was tiny, but I could express myself very well. Ann invited me to come round to CHES house right then. I immediately walked over there because I sensed I might be able to convince her that I was a perfect person for a scholarship. She asked me all kinds of questions and I opened myself up to her. Taking no time to hesitate, Ann decided that I should have a scholarship.

"I will take you down to Kisumu and buy you the clothes, shoes and books you need to go to secondary school," Ann announced. "Can you go now and tell your Mother? Then come back tomorrow and we will go shopping."

"Yes, of course. This is an answer to my prayer, Ann. Thank you, thank you."

"Do you have any relatives or friends that live close to Ekambuli School? You need to live with someone near the school. It is too far to travel everyday from your Mother's *shamba*."

"I have an Aunt. I will talk to her before I return home today," I said excitedly.

I hurried to my Aunt's house and told her my good news. Auntie's eyes lit up.

"Of course, my house is here for you to stay in. Now go quickly home because night will be soon. Here is some money for the *matatu*."

Because I couldn't safely be on the roads after dark, I ran to catch the *matatu* by the store. As always, it was crammed with people. I shoved my way through the door and eased my tiny body through the narrow space between two rows of double seats, filled with twelve people. I then sat on the edge at the end of the rear seat. The vehicle lurched off down the red dirt road as I hunched on the seat, my soul singing with hope.

When I reached our farm, I searched for my Mother in the fields of yam plants.

"Mother, I have such good news! When I took my cousin's books to his school, God opened a door for me. I can go to secondary school. CHES will pay my fees. Ann, the Agent, is taking me to Kisumu tomorrow to buy everything I need for Form One."

"Oh, Everlyne, such an opportunity for you! You will work hard now that the Lord has sent someone to help you. You must graduate from secondary school. Make something of yourself. I am so happy for our family. You will be able to get a job and bring money home to make our life better."

Next morning I rose at 5:30 a.m., bathed and dressed in my one good dress. I could barely eat the *ugi*, the maize porridge, my Mother had prepared for me. I was so excited. I ran to catch the *matatu* to travel to CHES house. Ann was waiting for me in the living room.

"Come, we must hurry to catch the 8:10 departure."

We absolutely ran as fast as we could, our bags flopping in the breeze. Ann stopped at the back of the van, eaten with rust, and checked its tires.

"The tires are not too bald," she remarked quietly. "I think they will get us to Kisumu."

We climbed into the *matatu* and shoved our way to the back where we would not be bothered by people getting on. I spent the whole ride with my eyes on the scene flying by us. One of the things I will never forget is when I saw the "weeping rock" for the very first time. I had heard the story about it so I was so eager to share it with Ann.

"Ann, do you see that rock over there weeping?"

"Yes. It is that very tall grey rock looking like a giant sausage towering on the hillside. See that narrow stream of water runing constantly down from the top of the rock to the ground," Ann noted, as she stared out the window.

"I will tell you the story of why it is so," Everlyne said. "A long time ago the Maasai warriors were fighting the Luyha men right here. It was a terrible battle, leaving all the Luyha warriors dead. From that day on, the large boulder has never stopped weeping for the loss of those men."

"Everlyne, I will remember this story every time I see that rock in the field."

Within an hour, we were smoking down the hill into Kisumu. We spent the whole day there—my first visit in the city perched on Lake

Victoria. The main street seemed so wide and the stores and government buildings were painted, not covered with mould like in Kakamega.

"What are those dome-shaped roofs?"

"Mosques," Ann replied, "for the Muslim Asians who run so many of the businesses here. Many Asians, from India have lived in this town since the late 1800's."

We walked down the main street towards Lake Victoria and turned right—onto the street where we could buy uniforms. As we walked along, I told Ann Lake Victoria was so large that it touched not only Kenya, but also Uganda and Tanzania. We reached the shop that sold school clothes. A bell tinkled our entrance. Anne led me to the rack of school uniforms. I loved the navy-blue skirt and pullover. The white blouse was crisp and new—not like the second-hand clothes I usually wore. I felt so proud when she paid for my uniform. Then, a few doors up we bought a pair of shoes and white stockings. Getting the books, pens, geometry set and notebooks took us into many shops until at last we had everything I needed. The day was very hot—over 30 degrees Centigrade on the circular thermometer hanging on the outside of the pharmacy—and extremely humid. My blouse was damp and stuck to my back.

"Let's go for lunch," Ann suggested, wiping the sweat from her fore-head. "If you feel like me, you could use something to drink. Come, we will go to the Grill House Restaurant and you can try a hamburger, fries and juice. Would you like that?"

"Yes! This has to be a perfect day. I have never had so many new things in all my life."

"Well, I want you always to remember that CHES is helping you—so you can help others."

"Oh, I will. I promise."

That night I stayed with my Aunt so I could go to school the next day. The first term had started and I didn't want to miss any more classes. Before I went to bed, I printed my name on all my new notebooks and put everything carefully in my new school bag.

Next morning I left my Aunt's house before seven o'clock to get to school early. I wanted to walk around the inside of the building to get familiar with the rooms where my classes would be. Before school began, I went into the Principal's office to get a timetable. He welcomed me warmly to Ekambuli.

The classes slipped by, as if I was in a dream. At the end of the day, Ann was there. "How did your day go?' she asked.

"Perfect! I am so happy to be here," I replied.

"Good. Here is some paraffin for a lamp at your Aunt's house. You will need to use it for light so that you can study every evening after supper."

"I will. I want to get good marks. Thank you so much. You have opened a new road for my life now."

Little did I know at that moment when she gave me the paraffin what hurdles would face me at my Aunt's house. Auntie used all my paraffin to cook with that night, and on every following night that I received it from Ann. She also made me work before I went to school. When I came home I had to collect wood, go for water, pick vegetables, and cook dinner before I washed up. It was late when I finally was able to open my schoolbag to get out my assignments. My Aunt always had used my paraffin up so I couldn't do my reading or writing in the dark. We began to quarrel all the time. Then she stopped supplying breakfast because my Mother wasn't paying her anything.

When I told Ann about the situation, she provided enough food for my breakfast. But the situation continued to be very difficult with my Aunt, so Ann arranged my transfer to Matende Secondary School during Form One. From CHES funds, Ann paide the entire fee of 2700 Shillings to the school.

This was 1990, and I proved that perseverance paid off. My Mother had so often told me, when I was younger, that if I kept working hard, then success would visit me. Now I knew it to be true. I liked my new school. Ann told me I had adjusted so well because I had a teachable spirit. I knew I constantly looked at the positive side and worked very hard—even during the holidays. There was always someone there to help me whenever I needed support. For example, the geography teacher at Matende Secondary School, who lived in Kabras with her child, realized I needed accommodation. She called and told me she would provide room and board. I went to stay with her. Very soon, she began to call me her daughter. We are still friends today.

But, during Form Four, something happened. I shut down. I felt depressed and I still don't know why. I think I didn't see a future for myself after secondary school. Other students, my teachers, and even my Uncle encouraged me. They told me I was smart. The Deputy Principal nurtured me. She was friendly and gave me moral support. We were like mother and child. Also, my sponsor was so loving and kind in her letters to me and always included a little extra money. I saw my future brighten when my sponsor said she would fund the next step of my education. She told me to choose between a secretarial and tailoring course after I received my Kenya Certificate of Secondary Education (K.C.S.E.). In 1994, when the results of the K.C.S.E. were publicized, I achieved a C+ average on my final examinations. I did not get high enough marks to go to university or into nursing. I think I didn't do well on my exams because I had been ill. As a result I had to give up my dream of university. My family agreed with my sponsor that I should go to secretarial or tailoring school. I preferred being a secretary to making clothes. I had done the Home/Science course at secondary school so I knew how to sew. I was determined that I wasn't going to be a tailor.

I went to A.C.C.E.S., which was not too far from the CHES house, and they accepted me for a scholarship. With A.C.C.E.S. and my sponsor's help I went for two and a half years to a secretarial course that involved computer training at Imara Commercial College in Kakamega. I lived on my own in one room in a house that I had rented for a 1,000 Shillings from my secondary school teacher of Geography. A.C.C.E.S. gave me enough money to cover the rent and living expenses for each year. I sold *mandazas,* deep-fried doughouts, with my brother to buy kerosene for the *jiko* and the stove. I liked living on my own and using my own money to keep myself independent.

Unfortunately I became sick again before the third stage of my studies at Imara College was finished and, in 1997, I was forced to terminate my studies at the secretarial college because of these health problems. When I was feeling better I needed a job to get some money to survive on. I went to Busia and taught secretarial studies for three months at Bumba Technical School. When the Principal found he had no funds to pay me, the staff paid my salary because they appreciated that I had stood in for the teacher who was on leave.

When I finished at Bumba, I knew it would be very hard to survive without money coming in each month. I decided to leave Busia and go back to Kakamega to see if I could volunteer at CHES house while I looked for another job. Again a stroke of bad luck overturned my world. Someone stole my purse when I was helping out at CHES. But my world became bright when the Agent said, "You can stay here and do some work for us. We'll pay you 1,000 Shillings."

That money allowed me to finish stage three of my secretarial course at Imara Commerical College by 1998. Before the Agent returned to Canada, she persuaded the A.C.C.E.S. Agent to take me on—after I finished my course at college. My brother-in-law, who passed away a year later, assisted me with accommodation, but I had little money for other things. Those were hard times.

After completing my course work, the A.C.C.E.S Agent needed an assistant in the office to help her. She asked me to come and work half-time at A.C.C.E.S. I started immediately and have been here ever since. In 2000, I started to work full time as the Executive Secretary for A.C.C.E.S. and to look after the Student Scholarship Programme.

At present, I am 25 years old. I married my husband two years ago. Last year I bought a piece of property to build my own house. We are saving money and buying materials to build a house on the property this fall. Right now, we live in a rented house just beyond where the CHES house is, in Lurambee area. Our goal is to be in our own new house by Christmas this year. My daughter, Glory, is seven months old now. I pay a ten year old girl to baby-sit her while I work here everyday.

I have had many successes in my life. I am proud of my position of Executive Secretary with A.C.C.E.S. I am proud of the two Canadian organizations—A.C.C.E.S. and CHES. Both organizations challenge many Kenyan parents to understand that a girl can be educated and helpful in the community. Women can move beyond what parents believe and expect women to do. Most parents who are farmers think girls should sit at home and take care of the children. With education, some females are beginning to realize they can work at a job in the community and earn their own money. In addition, I feel very privileged to meet the Canadian volunteers who come to Kakamega. These Canadians make me and other Kenyans feel hopeful. They are kind and supportive. They talk to us and give us presents and money when we are in need.

I am the only one in my family who has graduated so far. I supported my older brother, who had dropped out of school, until he finished his secondary education. He is now a second year student at Western University taking a Diploma in Mechanical Engineering. Two of my sisters lost their husbands to illnesses. So I help support them and also my Mother. I opened a small business of selling notions for them to become self-supportive. I assist my family as much as I can, just as I encourage my friends. I even give gifts of money to my close friends. I believe that, in being assisted, I must help others.

But I want to be self-sufficient. It is my house and my property. If my husband leaves or dies, I will still have my home and my job so I'll always have an income. That is so important to me. I was brought up in a bigamist family. I don't want to go through what my Mother did. I won't. I am hardworking and determined. Although my husband has been laid-off from his job, I still believe unity is power. You know, two is better than one. I have targets to achieve, like my house and opening a business for my husband. I will get them all. I am a woman of the new world of Kenya."

As darkness falls, Everlyne switches off the tape recorder. Delighted she has finished with her past she locks up and walks to her home.

Everlyne Musalia

Ambitious and determined,

Striving to reach her own goals in modern Kenyan life.

A Kenyan woman who values her independence,

She is driven never to repeat the past.

Proud of her work as secretary of A.C.C.E.S. Kenya.

❖ *Francis Butichi*

itting across the table is an elegant man in his late twenties. We are having lunch at the Golf Club in Kakamega because Francis told me on the phone that morning he had an important announcement to share. As he carefully nibbles his beef curry stew and rice, using a knife and fork, rather than his hands as is the custom here, I note his deep navy business suit. It is highlighted by a crisp white shirt and a blue and ochre striped tie. His dark brown eyes glitter with excitement as we talked about his job as the A.C.C.E.S. coordinator of eight rural schools in poverty-stricken areas of Western Province.

The conversation pauses for a change as Francis pushes back his empty plate with the silverware neatly angled on it.

"Well, I have some big news," he says. "I have got a one year contract job with the Lutheran World Federation as Senior Education Officer. My work will be at the Kakuma Refugee Camp in Turkana District, northwest Kenya. The camp has over 83,000 refugees from all over Africa."

"What a promotion. I am definitely impressed. When are you going?"

"I'll leave Kakamega on January 4th."

"Have you told anyone else?"

"I've written a resignation letter to A.C.C.E.S. in Canada. I am meeting our local Executive Board to finalize the 2004 plans and hand over the organization to the next person. I finish at the end of the December."

"What incredible news, Francis. Such recognition of your accomplishments with A.C.C.E.S. and the primary literacy centers, your intellect and hard work. Well done."

I lean across the table and firmly shake Francis' hand. A large grin creases his face and his eyes beam with pride.

"I'm so happy for you," I say. "You deserve this job, but A.C.C.E.S. will miss your talents."

"I want to tell you how much I appreciated all the prepping you did with me for the interview," Francis states. "It made such a difference."

"I enjoyed it," I said, my smile matching his grin.

"Now, I want to hear something about your background" I say. "You sit opposite to me, looking like a person born to a wealthy family."

"Quite the contrary," Francis states, raising his eyebrows.

"Well, I am all ears. Where did you start out in life?"

"I am a Luyha, born in Eldoret. Father worked there. My Mother and Father had a big disagreement after the fourth child was born. I don't know what about. My Mother took all four of us, my older sister, me and my younger brother and sister, to live with her Mother, my maternal Grandmother, in Musoli."

"Did your Grandmother live alone?"

"No, she had two sons at home, as well as two of my Mother's sisters and their four grown children. She supported all of us."

"How did she support all of these members of her family?"

"She had a *shamba,* a small farm, where she grew maize, cassava, arrowroot, yams and potatoes. We grew up on lots of carbohydrates. *Uji* porridge for breakfast and lunch. Then *ugali,* which is ground maize cooked in water and beaten smooth, and potatoes or cassava for supper. She also produced *Chang'Aa,* a rough, alcoholic beer, made from maize, and sold it."

"What were the living conditions at your Grandmother's place?"

"The usual thatched hut. We had three rooms and a kerosene light and stove. There were no beds or mattresses. We each had a sugar sack to lie on and a piece of blanket to cover us. Grandmother had cut one big blanket up into sections and we each got our part. In the mornings we would roll up our blankets and place them in a sugar sack that hung on the back of a door."

"What did your Mother do?"

"Before I went to Primary School, my Mother left for Nairobi to get a job. She stayed there and re-married. She had two more kids. We never saw her during that time."

"How did your Grandmother cope with all that responsibility?"

"She made us work hard. We had to graze the cows, fetch water, and gather bits of firewood—the kind of jobs only the girls were supposed to do. I also had to work for someone else to get money. I was hated at my Grandmother's house because I was left there by my Mother. Also, I was defiant.

As I got older, I helped my Grandmother with the *Chang'Aa.* My Grandmother used the beer that she brewed to give drinks to everyone in the house, including the children. Everyone one, except me. I never drank any, but all the others in the house drank. They each were given a share, enough to get drunk and fall asleep. Then they forgot about their hunger. I refused ever to drink alcohol or beer because I could see what harm it caused. I disagreed with my Grandmother all the time. She and her sons and other daughters hated me. I was beaten so many times. I remember after Standard One, which is the same as your Grade One, someone at my Grandmother's house didn't like me at all. I don't recall who that was. As a result I couldn't eat or read at the table."

"So, you did go to Primary School?" I ask softly.

"I started young. I was five. I was a tiny child, even in secondary school. It wasn't until after high school that I grew to my present five feet, ten inches."

"What do you remember about your early school life?"

"I think I was bright. By Standard Two, when I was six, I was reading books, magazines, anything I could get my hands on. I spoke three languages—my tribal Luyha language called Kiluyha which I learned in my Grandmother's village, our national Kiswahili so I could talk to all the people from different tribes, and English—a left-over from the British time in Kenya. These last two languages I learned at school. I loved school. It was the only way to get away from the work at home, and the bleak situation. I was bright and assertive. If I thought something was not good, I would say so. I would refuse to do things. Then my Grandmother would beat me. At school, the teachers were friendly— genuine people who liked me. I enjoyed learning and teachers always appreciated that. I loved school for the learning it provided and for taking me away from home."

"As children from Eldoret, how did you fit into the village life?"

"My siblings and I were discriminated against. The village people called us 'children of girls' because my Mother had brought us to live at Grandmother's house. Culturally we were branded.

I won a Presidential Award for academic achievement at school, but I didn't receive it because we didn't belong to the village. On my part, I did not want to be like the other boys in the village. They were not interested in school or in changing their lives."

"How did you do on your final exams in Primary School?"

"Though I had performed the best in my class, I did poorly on the K.C.S.E., the Kenya Certificate of Standard Examinations. Those are Kenya's countrywide final tests every student must take and pass. I think

I had lost hope that I would ever go to secondary school. My Grandmother told me to go to work after Standard Eight. She would not pay my fees for secondary school because she was paying for my two young Uncles' school fees. I had been selected by the school to be one of four students to be considered for a CHES scholarship. Three of this group received their scholarships, but I did not. I was never sure whether I was not selected because of the exam results or whether my assertive ways were not liked at school either."

"So what did you do?"

"Well, my older sister, Margaret, had received a CHES scholarship in the previous year and had gone to Imbale Secondary School. My primary school's Head Master encouraged me to go to Imbale. He wrote the Agent at CHES and the Principal of Imbale Secondary School. That Head Master was a real "change agent" for me. I thought, then, that with the letter, maybe things would change. I knew, ever since I was a young boy, I wanted to have better opportunities than my family. What happened was the CHES Agent told me if I did well in the first term, then I could get a scholarship. The Principal of Imbale let me attend the first term without paying. In the end, I received the CHES scholarship when one of the three who had been awarded a scholarship didn't show up for school opening."

"How did you do at Imbale Secondary School?"

"I worked hard to prove to my Canadian sponsor I could do well. CHES monies paid for my uniform and books. By Form Three, like your Grade Eleven, I paid my own fifteen percent required by CHES, plus the annual fifteen percent required for my sister, Margaret, and for my desk-mate, Alfred. I did this by my own work. I grew and sold *sukuma*, the green leafy vegetable like bitter spinach. I brewed and sold *Chang'Aa*. I had lots of energy and was driven by the reality that my Grandmother wouldn't give me any money. There was no one else to help me. I wasn't going to sit there and wait for help. I had no shoes until Form Three— when I was about sixteen years old. I planted a crop of *sukuma* and sold it to pay for my first pair of shoes. What a surprise when I found out my CHES sponsor had sent money for shoes at that very same time. So I went from nothing to two pairs of shoes."

"Did you ever hear from your Mother in Nairobi?"

"My Mother moved back to Kakamega with her two children when I was in secondary school. I left my Grandmother's house and moved in with my Mother by Form Two. I was the only one of us four children to join her then. I stayed with her until the end of Form Four of secondary school."

"How was your relationship with your Mother?"

"When she left us alone with my Grandmother, I felt abandoned. But, as a child, what could I do? It was made so much worse by the way my Grandmother treated me. I felt she really didn't want me in her house. I knew my Father was an able man and was respected in Eldoret, but he didn't want anything to do with me either. My Mother has never told us why they broke up and why she left the matrimonial home. My Uncles and Grandmother mistreated my Mother as well as us. They ignored her completely. I felt sorry for her. After she left for Nairobi and I later heard that she had married again, I felt so confused and upset. When Mother was with us at Grandmother's, I used to work with her on the farms. I even did that when I moved in with her during the time I went to secondary school. I don't know why my younger brothers and my elder sister didn't join us then, but they didn't. Even I found staying with her was difficult.

During university, I lived with my younger brother in Kakamega on break times. I paid part of his rent. Later I wanted to do something for my Mother. I built her a house and bought her a dairy cow. The cow produces milk with which she feeds her two children and herself. She sells the rest. I now pay part of her two new children's fees for school. At the present moment she is happy and content. I feel happy because she is also. I think my Mother loved me. She is the only person, I believe, who has genuinely loved me. I see the improvement of my Mother's life as my greatest success."

"How did you first hear about A.C.C.E.S.?"

"In Form Two or Three, the Head Master at Imbale called all the CHES students together and told us to perform well so that we could get a scholarship to university. Before he talked to us, none of us had ever imagined going to university. I, like the others, worked very hard then to achieve that goal."

"And you received an A.C.C.E.S. scholarship. Did you always want to be a teacher?"

"Yes. I was called for a Bachelor of Arts at Kenyatta University in Nairobi, but A.C.C.E.S. was only going to fund students going for Bachelors of Education because there was a great need in Kenya for new teachers. So I changed my program to a Bachelor of Education."

"Going to university in Nairobi must have been a big change."

"No, I was used to Nairobi. I had been in Nairobi every holiday during my secondary school years. During that time, I was brewing and selling *Chang'Aa*. I used to sell it in Nairobi because I could get a better price. But going to university was different for me. The first year I felt inferior and real loneliness. It took me time to come to terms with others. Everyone was new. I couldn't trust anybody else. I don't know why—when I look back on it now. I had no friends because all of them had gone to other universities. So I went to the library for books and then worked in my room. Even now I do this.

However, I made friends in the second year and I socialized with people of different cultures. I would meet friends for coffee. I was very comfortable with university life then. But, still, I spent eighty percent of my time just reading and studying. On my breaks I started a business of selling t-shirts in Kakamega and that tied me over after graduation for a few months—until a job came up with A.C.C.E.S. You know, I thought my Grandmother would be proud of me at last, proud that someone in her family had graduated from university, but it is only just recently that she is."

"After university, what did you do?"

"I had a dream in my last year of university that I would create something for me to do, something in which I could see results happening. In 1998, Alinda Ware, at CHES, hired me to do a survey on the number of children not going to school in Kakamega District. When I finished the task and wrote my report, she shared it with Beth and George Scott, of A.C.C.E.S. The key finding of the research was that many poor children in the rural areas of Kakamega were not attending school. Hearing those results, Beth and George wanted something done to get more children to school.

I worked with the A.C.C.E.S. Agent to develop the first literacy center. I had two volunteers from Canada help me—Jay Procktor, a young teacher, and Floyd Harry, a retired Canadian Principal. Floyd has been my consultant at the other end of e-mails ever since. We found one community church out in one of the poorest areas of subsistence farms. The community let us use their church for a school. Imbale Literacy Centre was born. We started then with parent involvement and A.C.C.E.S. funded this school. Their donations hired the teachers and paid for the learning materials. We named Imbale the first L.I.F.A. Center. L.I.F.A. means "Literacy For All" which is the founding belief that initiated this project. Every child in Kenya should have an education."

"You started that first L.I.F.A. (Literacy for All) center only three years ago and now there are eight. Tell me how you did that," I probe.

"I was hired by A.C.C.E.S. to supervise and coordinate the opening of two Literarcy Centers at Isulu and Emukaba. I then started to develop a curriculum for student learning at the Centers. Independently, I coordinated the entire Literacy Project and opened more Centers at Munasio and Ematsayi.

A.C.C.E.S. funded the Literacy Projects at the centers and helped to move the L.I.F.A. organization into a formal C.B.O., Community Based Organization, by 2001. A.C.C.E.S. pays for the salaries of the present thirty-five teachers, the four of us in the office plus the accountant and the secretary. Also, they provide funds for some materials."

"That is a significant growth," I exclaim. "Thirty-five teachers have employment and seven people on the L.I.F.A. team in the office. Wow!"

"I used to work alone after the two volunteers left and do everything. I tried so hard to work with the people in the communities. It was a challenge to make this new idea of Literacy Centers successful. It was a foreign idea to the community, a totally new idea. The children's parents had never thought about sending their children to school to learn to read and write. They were resigned to their poverty.

Also, I was young. I was fresh out of university when I approached them. It wasn't easy. If I had been older, I automatically would have received respect. Since I am young, I had to earn it. That has been difficult, but we are making good progress."

"What a great accomplishment!"

"I think that I have been able to give back to our society the same help I have received. These children in the L.I.F.A. Centers are like me. I was once poor like them, without shoes or good clothes. Though it is little, I have made a great change in their lives."

"You have so much to be proud of," I comment quietly.

"I am proud of myself," Francis says and then he giggles. "I am proud of what I have achieved." More giggles. "When I look back on my childhood and when I compare myself to my age-mates who didn't go to school, I see that I am very different. I have achieved so much." Again, a gentle giggle.

"How different do you think you are after these three years of achievements?"

"I am more confident than I was three years ago. I can talk with anyone. I realize I know many things, but I want to pursue more. I have learned from my readings in teacher research about the importance of studying and developing myself professionally. I am open to all opportunities to learn."

"So we have come back to where we started this conversation," I reflect. "How do you feel about your accomplishments to date?"

"I feel proud. My people need me," Francis responds strongly. "I have used my skills to help my people. I am happy to be able to do that."

"Well, Francis, that says it all, doesn't it?"

Francis grins, his smile like a large crescent moon in a dark African sky.

Francis Butichi

Ambitious and hard-working.

Highly intelligent and articulate Kenyan who developed rural schools

And now, as a new Director, is moving to shape a refugee camp,

Much larger and more challenging.

A man with success as his mantle and sensitivity as his sword.

A man well-travelled on the road to making a difference in people's lives.

Francis at my farewell dinner

Lifa school children

✜ Justine Mutoberra

*J*ustine is a man whose reputation preceded him. When I arrived as a brand-new A.C.C.E.S. Agent in Kakamega, I heard about this man who was the organizing giant behind SAIPE, Students' AIDS Intervention and Prevention Education Programme. Justine organized this group when he was at university and developed an innovative programme of song, dance and drama for the group to present at sports and school events to raise community awareness of HIV and AIDS.

I got to know Justine personally within my first few weeks in Western Kenya. The other three Canadian volunteers and I were invited to Sunday lunch at Justine's home at the Muslim School compound in Mumias, a city near Kakamega. As is the Kenyan custom, we each brought a bag of sugar or flour as a gift to his wife. To host a meal for guests is an enormous undertaking financially for a family, even one that has the husband working.

After a forty minute journey in a *matatu*, a rusty mini-van with passengers packed like fish in a salmon boat, we reached the parking lot in the center of Mumias. Justine was waiting and took us across the street to the gated entrance of the Muslim School. He led us on a tour of the many low wooden buildings, all painted white, which comprised the school. We peeked into the boys' dormitory, an immense room filled with metal bunk-beds, before we reached his compact white staff house in a cluster of houses separating the girls' dormitory from the boys.

The four of us entered his small house that had electricity and water, but no indoor plumbing. The five of us filled all the seats on the couch and chairs in the small living room. His wife, Linet, came into the room and welcomed us to their home. While the rest of us talked, she produced a meal of chicken stew, *ugali and sukuma wiki*—which is cooked ground maize served with a dark green bitter chard, roasted potatoes, and fried *matoke*—large green bananas called plantains. After, I talked with Justine separately as we walked outside around the compound. It was then I decided I wanted to get to know him better.

A few weeks later we sat down and talked. Justine articulately answered my questions about his life in an easy, forthright manner that seemed a second skin for him.

"In my life, luck has been mixed with sorrow. But I have always been aware of my desire to help others. I think it began when I was a small boy. My family lived in the Manyasa area on a small farm, *shamba,* with a hut for my grandparents and another one for my parents. Each hut, *banda,* was the traditional two-room, round, mud-walled hut with a grass thatched roof.

As the eldest child and first-born son, I slept with my grandparents in their hut. We were poor, but I felt so loved by my grandparents and my Father and Mother that poverty did not loom as an important spectre in my life. My earliest memories of those days were centered upon my Grandfather telling me stories about his life and our ancestors. He made the past come alive with detailed descriptions about how our Luyha tribe had helped others. These tales became very relevant to my life because they showed me that being good at what I did would bring success.

My Father, who was a farmer, took only one wife. This was contrary to the Luyha's tribal customs of a man marrying several women to produce a multitude of children to increase his status and that of the tribe. However, my Mother had nine children with my Father, so he had prestige in our village.

During my childhood, our family went without many things— enough so that I can remember days where there was no food for lunch or supper. Sometimes we would go to a neighbour to ask for extra bananas or yams. Many times they had none to share.

On those nights we would drink lots of water to still the hunger wracking our stomachs. It was traditional that neighbours helped one another when they could. In supporting each other, we stayed alive. Our family, in turn, would assist others when their food ran short in the Long Rains season. In the Short Rains season that normally ran from August to April, the thunderstorms shook the sky everyday, usually in the late afternoon. Rains helped the maize, beans, yams and potatoes to grow to be harvested. Some days during this season had no rain. The new set of crops was planted well before the Long Rains began in April. In the Long Rains season, the rain each day would be longer and we would shiver at night with the cold. In Mumias we were at an altitude of five thousand feet so the nights were very chilly. During the Long Rains our high altitude affected the growth of crops. Families like ours had to depend on good growing conditions. Sometimes we ran out of maize or beans before the season of the Short Rains finished its cycle and the plants were harvested. That is when we had to help each other.

When I was six, I went to Standard One in our village school. By the second year I was reading. I don't recall how my Father paid my school fees—perhaps he was able to get one of my Uncles to help out. I was a quiet, dedicated student through those years and I studied long hours. Working hard was a strong value in our family. I had seen the adults of my family putting a lot of time and energy into farming and running the household. I just did my studies the way everyone else worked.

Around my seventh year in school, I spent a long time talking to a neighbour, a very religious man, about my desire to become a priest. He encouraged me to attend St. Peter's Seminary, in Mukumu, so I could enter the priesthood. This school was a long way from my home and the fees were costly. I didn't believe I would have a chance to go to any secondary school. When I received 480 out of the 600 marks on the final examination in Standard Eight, St. Peter's Catholic Secondary School offered me a bursary for the entire four years. My Father borrowed money to pay for my uniforms and books. It was very important to my Father that the first-born son have an opportunity of attending secondary school to improve the family status.

Only one glitch nearly derailed the starting of my new life. The priest at St. Peter's didn't inform us about an important intake interview into the seminary at the Catholic Church until one evening, just twelve hours before the interview. Feeling overwhelming panic that I might miss this interview, I caught the overnight bus. I made it on time. And I was accepted.

During my secondary years, one family in my village made a big impact on me and my future. The two sons in this family were in university and became role models for me. I admired those two fellows so much. When I came home on school breaks, I always went over to the family's farm. I liked the clothes the young men wore, the way they behaved, and, especially, the respect and recognition the community gave each of them. I always heard people talking about the hard work and successes of these two men. I wanted to be like them. I realized I must go to university to achieve my goal of living a life like my heroes. At the same time, I discovered within myself the priesthood was not for me. Instead, I wanted to go to university so I could be educated as a teacher and help others to better their lives.

I stayed in residence at the secondary school and spent much time in preparing for the tests and examinations. In my last year there, one teacher told me that everyone on staff thought I was an exemplary student.

I passed Form Four with a 'B' which meant I was accepted into a university. Excitement flooded my soul because my future now had a possibility of success. All I needed was the funds. Luck danced upon my life again a short time later. During the two "gap" years between finishing secondary school and starting university, I met, by chance, an old man. He described how his daughter was applying to A.C.C.E.S., a Canadian organization in Kakamega that provided scholarships for bright students to go to university. He explained that A.C.C.E.S. considered poor men and women, like me, who had graduated from secondary school with excellent marks.

The next day as I caught a *matatu* to the A.C.C.E.S. office, I practiced silently what I was going to say to persuade the Agent I was a worthy candidate. *My family had a subsistence farm to live on, with no outside income. I had seven brothers and a sister. As the eldest, the family was dependent on me to get an education so that I could get an income-paying job. I had always achieved good marks at school and I worked hard to be successful. I promised myself that if I was helped by A.C.C.E.S., then I would assist others, wherever possible.*

The sun danced on the dark green leaves and the deep red flowers on the flame trees as the *matatu* zipped along the road to Kakamega. My confidence in the future shone out from inside me as I knocked on the door of the A.C.C.E.S. house. I was invited in. The Agent explained the scholarship program to me and asked me a lot of questions about my family and school life. My answers seemed to satisfy her and she accepted me for a scholarship. At this point, I felt like shouting with joy. I knew at that moment I would finish university and be like my two heroes.

Shortly after, I went off to Kenyatta University in Nairobi to start my Bachelor of Education in Science. Adjusting to the life at the university in our large capital city was a major process. At the seminary in Mumias, the other students were friendly and the teachers and the priests maintained close, warm relations with each student. They cared about us as learners and human beings. On the other hand, students at Kenyatta University were left on their own to struggle to survive in a vastly different milieu. The classes were large. The professors didn't recognize students and had no personal interest in us. We struggled to find enough to eat, and we had to study late into each night to keep up with the course work. Many of my peers fell into the drug, alcohol or sex scene, but I never joined them. I held in my mind the models of the two young men from my village when I was faced with making choices. I knew my family's future depended on me. I decided for myself I had to maintain an inner toughness to keep myself from that negative life style if I was to be successful. I really worked at my studies and maintained an A standing for three years. By the end of the third year, I was one of the hundred students recognized as a Top Performer on the Dean's List. I was proud and happy to be one of the best from the five thousand students who were attending the university. I had friends, sad to say, that ended up as failures and drunkards at Kenyatta University.

While I attended university I joined a group of Peer Educators who were trained by Path-Finder International. Several of us from Butere-Mumias were asked to conduct a study to find out what was ailing our two communities. We formalized our group under the name of Action AIDS. In our base-line study we attempted to find out about the rates of AIDS-related deaths and the impact of HIV and AIDS-related diseases through interviews, questionnaires and observations. Our findings revealed the immense impact that AIDS-related illnesses were having on people and their lives in the communities.

In Mumias, from this data, the rate of HIV infection among the adults was estimated to be around forty percent. This information was used to develop our Action Plan about HIV and AIDS-related diseases that we knew was causing so many deaths. At that time HIV was not being officially recognized as a disease by the Kenyan government.

In 1997, when I was in my third year as a student at Kenyatta University, our Action AID group formed an organization that we called SAIPE, to assist others to become informed about HIV and AIDS-related diseases. I was the founder of SAIPE. I became very active in the group and I talked about HIV and its prevention to other students. We decided to start our campaign at the university with our student colleagues. We put on plays to catch the attention of these youth.

SAIPE carried out a baseline study during August 1998 among selected schools and churches. We targeted 200 people in youth groups, women's groups and cultural groupings in Mumias and Matungu. The research revealed a high level of ignorance of knowledge on HIV and AIDS. From the study, eighty-six percent of the respondents were aware of HIV/AIDS but most expressed distorted, judgmental and stigmatizing facts about the disease ravaging our people in the community. To the

Elders, HIV/AIDS was not a new phenomenon. They said it had been there before. Others of the community felt it was witchcraft and they sought the traditional healer's intervention. Some Christians looked upon the HIV/AIDS clients as sinners and cursed. A cluster of individuals believed faith in God was a cure to AIDS. Some Christians campaigned against the use of condoms, saying it encouraged immorality.

Twenty-five percent of the youth interviewed were not well informed about basic HIV/AIDS prevention. This data was worrying since 1.5 million young people in Kenya became sexually active every year. Sixty-five percent of the youth interviewed had more than one boy-girl relationship and seventy-five percent never used condoms while having sex. At the time, there was no widely orchestrated program dealing with the youth and HIV/AIDS.

In 1999, SAIPE became active in Butere-Mumias. We used theatre participation, songs, music and dance at sports events, particularly soccer, which is called football in Africa, to educate the public about HIV. Before this time the adults in our communities had not heard about HIV and the diseases related to AIDS.

One day, we invited the General Manager, and his wife, of Mumias Sugar Company to a football tournament. Our group sang a never-ending song about the need for men to bring home bread, not AIDS, to the family. They sang and danced around and among the spectators who were mainly men and boys. Our hope was that these males become familiar with the words HIV and AIDS and ask others about it meaning. We needed to start people talking about this dreaded disease. Kenyans still do not speak about HIV, what sexual practices are the causes of this disease, and what men need to do to prevent bringing the virus home to their wives. The statistic in Kenya is that eighty-five percent of married women who remain faithful to their partner get the HIV virus from their husbands. That has to be changed and that is what we slowly will do.

I maintained that high level of personal commitment to SAIPE as well as my studies. I graduated, in October, 1998, and I had my first teaching job in January, 1999, as a voluntary Science teacher at Theresia Secondary School in Bumini. I took this position because I realized the Kenyan government was not hiring teachers at this time.

The students in my very first class at Theresia performed well on the final examination, achieving a 5.4 mean score. This was the school's best performance on the Science examination to that point in time, so I received high recognition from educators and parents for my teaching ability. I consider this one of my personal bests. Unfortunately, my position came to an end as the teacher who had been away returned to his assignment.

I then traveled to Mombasa because I heard there were some openings in teaching. Unfortunately I arrived one day late for the interviews so that possibility fell through the grate—like a piece of ash from the fire. When I returned to Mumias, St. Mary's Secondary School immediately offered me a job as a Science teacher, at the same time as the government advertised they were holding interviews at Mumias Muslim School. I wanted the security of a government teaching position so I went for the interview at the Muslim School. I was picked as the best teacher candidate in August 2001, and taught Science to secondary students and lived in the accommodation provided on site.

At the same time, I continued my work with SAIPE. A new dimension emerged in our HIV work. The challenge of children, orphaned by their parents dying from AIDS, emerged. Their stories had a familiar pattern. Father became thin and tired. Then he became sick with a variety of diseases and died. Very quickly, Mother followed his pattern. When this first started happening to husbands and wives, the other relatives—aunts, uncles, grandparents—would take the children into their homes. As the disease began to affect many couples in a family, the other relatives did not have enough food, space or money to house the little ones. Soon, it started that, after the mother's funeral, the children in this situation had no place to go to be cared for and so they remained all alone in their Mother and Father's hut. They harvested the crop and begged for seeds to plant the next crop. Sometimes they left their *shamba* or were forced out by people who seized their land. Then they went into the town to live.

In 2000, our town of Mumias began to have growing numbers of homeless orphans from the countryside. They picked-up leftover fruits from the streets and vegetables from the market's dump as they wandered aimlessly in the dusty streets. They were filthy and their clothes dirty and ragged. Sometimes a person from a restaurant would give them scraps of food, or the orphans would steal to survive. SAIPE decided they would tackle the problem of orphans that had moved into our community. We asked the residents for food, clothing and families to offer shelter to these bereft children. We mobilized the community to take all these small children to live within their extended families. My wife and I have one orphan living with us now.

In 2001 a man from the United States came to Mumias to take a look at what we were doing. He was happy with our community initiative and set up a fund to take care of thirteen families who had taken in orphans. He paid their school fees so these children could go to school. He also provided money for income-generating activities for the adults of the families hosting the orphans. One family bought a cow that would produce milk for sale in the community. Another mother bought a sewing machine to tailor clothes. A Canadian volunteer teacher assisted three more children. Two of the original group of orphans are now in secondary school, with their school fees paid by the American. By September 2003, we had changed the lives of sixty-five orphans.

At the same time, as we worked to assist and change the lives of orphans, SAIPE continued to grow from its humble beginnings into an organization that is now many miles from where it started. Up to September 2003, we had presented our song, music and dance routines to one hundred community functions in schools, churches, market-places, sports events and public functions. However, when we presented our awareness sessions under a tree at the Chief's Center at the Shandi Market, we were harassed by the police. They wanted to know why we were there. We then had our planning meeting at our treasurer Earnest's home. In September 2002, we received 350,000 Shillings, nearly $6,000.00 Canadian, from the National Aids Control Council to continue our activities to build awareness of HIV within Mumias-Butere. We rented a small building so we could meet with people without harass-ment. In 2003, we received money from A.C.C.E.S. to buy office furniture for our small office. We also purchased a public communication system so our music and talks could be heard in the open-air places. Now, in our office we had the space to counsel individuals, hold our planning sessions, and conduct small workshops. At this time I don't need to assist SAIPE from my own pocket any more. In the summer of 2003 we received $55,000 Canadian dollars, through the work of a former A.C.C.E.S. agent, from the Canadian Teachers' Federation. We are in the process of enlarging our SAIPE offices in Shianda to include a room next door for a Resource Centre.

In January 2004, I facilitated at a SAIPE workshop on HIV/AIDS for teachers from the Butere-Mumias District. We planned a series of work-shops to train teachers in this area to develop lessons for the students to raise the awareness of HIV and to teach students how to prevent the disease from spreading.

My goal is clear. I want to be the top administrator at SAIPE while I continue to maintain my teaching position at the school. The teaching salary is secure, whereas funding of SAIPE varies. However, my hope is that SAIPE will be sustainable over time. Our goal is to develop SAIPE into an organization that is admired and recognized as a major player in the war against AIDS in Kenya. When it is consistently sustainable, then that will be the turning point where I can spend all my time working with SAIPE.

I realize that a person can't be successful alone. One must recognize others. My success story owes a lot to my parents, teachers, A.C.C.E.S., other friends who helped SAIPE, and donors from Europe and America, and also my wife. All these years Linet has gone without to make sure that SAIPE continues. She is always stable, positive and supportive. My own family has grown. My wife and I have a child. I also support one orphan and my sister-in-law. My wife has the job within SAIPE to work with the orphan families. I feel very fortunate.

My vision for the future is that SAIPE will have its own offices within a complex we have purchased. Youth will walk in and be counselled. The sick would receive medical attention in our fully-staffed clinic. Teacher training would be held in the hall which should be rented out when we were not using it. I will help SAIPE reach that dream so we can continue to help others. The A.C.C.E.S. circle of assisting others will become complete. I will make it happen."

Justine Mutoberra

Passionate and committed to reducing the incidence of HIV and the deaths by AIDS in his community.

An individual who is a model for others in how to help AIDS orphans.

A teacher who has gone beyond the classroom to touch other youth and adults.

A Kenyan designing a HIV Prevention program that is an example to others.

A success story.

Justine

Siepe presents songs, dancing and dramas to awareness of HIV/AIDS.

▨ *Philip Etende*

*P*hilip sits down beside the A.C.C.E.S. volunteer from Canada. His dark shining eyes twinkled—basking in her obvious respect. In his mid-thirties, Philip is wide-shouldered and stocky, his black hair cut short. He wears brown dress slacks and a crisply ironed plaid sports shirt.

"You were an excellent facilitator for our graduates' alumni meeting," the woman says, handing him a cup of milk tea and cookies.

"Thank you. I've had lots of experience."

"Well, we surely appreciated what you did today."

"Patrick, Everlyne, and I came up with the original idea of the CHES-A.C.C.E.S. Alumni Association, or C.A.A.A., as we now all call it?" he explains. "We wanted all the graduates who had received scholarships from CHES and A.C.C.E.S. to have an informal type of alumni, so we could meet together every year."

"How did you make it happen?"

"The three of us organized a meeting in the Kakamega Social Hall and informed the graduates. Lorrie Williams, the founder of CHES, gave us 2000 Shillings, less than $35.00 Canadian, to start. Later A.C.C.E.S. gave us a larger sum of money to assist our fledging organization to develop projects. I'm not only one of the original group, I am the oldest person in the organization."

Philip sips his tea and chews on sugar cookies and then begins his tale with an air of calm thoughtfulness.

"I was born, so many years ago, into a Luyha family in Ekambuli, far from the bustling town of Kakamega. My Father and Mother, who were traditional peasant farmers, struggled to survive as our family grew to include three children. Father had gone to Standard Four in school, so he was literate—not a common accomplishment for a farmer with one and a half acres of land. Mother planted maize and beans for our needs and sometimes there was enough so Father could sell what we didn't need to buy soap which we needed desperately. Soap was very important. We used it to wash ourselves, our clothes and our kitchen utensils.

Our family lived on our small farm, in a two-room mud-daub hut with a grass thatched roof, called a *banda*. It had one tiny room for the kitchen and another room, a bit larger, that we lived and slept in. Our hut was constructed in the traditional fashion. Young tree trunks were pounded into the ground to form a circle. More trunks were used to make a pointed roof skeleton. Thinner wood sticks were nailed or tied to the larger one to form the structure of the hut. Then the red earth was moistened with water and the mud smeared, or daubed, on, with the help of a few peoples' hands, over the wooden wall frame. Napier grass was used to make the roof. Our *banda* was like the thousands of huts that you still see scattered all over the green rolling hills around Kakamega. You call tell when a family has some extra money. Then the grass roof is replaced by iron sheet-metal.

Because I was the first-born and the only son, my Father took me to our church's Nursery School before I entered primary school. We sang songs, learned rhymes, letters and numbers, played games, and listened to the stories the teacher read to us. Father really wanted me to be educated. I was only able to go to school because my Father was employed at that time as a watchman at a school and could pay the fees for my primary education.

Before I was enrolled at primary school, the Head Teacher assessed me. She asked me to write my ABCs, do mathematical questions and draw designs. As a result, I went into Standard Two, equivalent to the North American Grade Two. Up to Standard Seven, my marks were in the top five, and sometimes I was first or second

During my primary school years, Father valued education so highly that he constructed a small hut near our main *banda* and equipped it with a paraffin lamp. I studied there in the quietness every evening. My sisters joined me there once my Father also sent them to school. Not all girls in our area had that opportunity, but Father paid the school fees for them because he believed in the education of girls. I think, as a peasant farmer, he was ahead of his time.

When I was 12 years old and ready to start secondary school, my Mother became seriously ill. That distressed me so much, but I didn't have much time to brood on my situation because I had to work hard on our farm to do my Mother's tasks, coming home everyday to prepare lunch for my sisters. To make things even tougher, my step-mother who was my Father's number two wife and lived in a *banda* close to us always quarreled with me. We never did get along, no matter how hard I tried. I missed the comfort of my Mother being in charge; the illness took a long time to go away. Eventually life returned to normal.

After achieving top grades on my final exams in primary school, I received my Certificate and was called to Butere Boys Secondary School. Father travelled to Nairobi to get assistance for the school fees from his cousin and an uncle who raised sugar cane. With their donations, he raised part of the fees for the first term. While he went to Nairobi, Mother took me to the Chief's office to request a bursary. We were turned down and I felt so bad. It looked as if my dream of joining secondary school was shattered. My Father decided he would go to see the Principal.

"We need the fees for the entire first term for Philip to come to classes," the Principal announced to my Father, who stood with his hat in his hands in front of the Principal's desk.

"I have raised all the money our family possibly can," my Father said quietly.

"Unfortunately it will not do. You must have money to come to our school," the Principal said loudly, smashing the hope that had glimmered on my Father's face. "Philip can join one of your relatives to learn mechanics or carpentry. Then he will be able to help support your family."

My discouraged Father scuffed up clouds of red dust as he plodded home. His dream that his only son would graduate from secondary school was falling apart.

A few days later, my former Primary Head Mistress sent a message with one of the Standard Six students that she wanted to see me. The next day I dashed to school and into her small office.

"Hello Philip," she said. "I hear you're having difficulty raising the fees for secondary school."

"Yes, we tried so hard, but we couldn't get enough."

"Are you still ready to learn?" she inquired.

"More than ever."

"Here, take this letter to Hector Sutherland, the Principal of Akambuli Secondary School. He will give you a chance," she said, handing me a long white envelope. "His Canadian friend, Lorrie Williams, will sponsor you."

"Thank you, Madame," I exclaimed. "You have made me full of hope. My Father will be so happy."

In 1982, the Principal, Mr. Sutherland, and the Canadian volunteer teacher, Lorrie Williams, made it possible for me to attend secondary school near where I lived. In fact, I was one of the first students Lorrie sponsored, before she formed CHES.

Because of the difficulties with the Principal at Butere Secondary School, I was late starting this new school. I began just before the first term's examinations. Even so, I had to take the tests and was dismayed at my results. I placed 72nd out of 186 students. I decided to aim for the top. I studied hard and for the rest of my years at the secondary school I was among the top five students. I wanted to be a teacher so much that I practiced it at secondary school. When there wasn't a teacher in our class, I taught until one arrived. The staff really appreciated that. At the end of Form Four, like your Grade Twelve, I took the Kenya-wide examinations and scored a Division One, which is the same as an A today. My dream became a possibility.

People in my family were overjoyed, but I was not. I was scared because some people in my village were hostile towards high-achieving school graduates. They would taunt and beat-up guys like me who did well. I had only one solution. I hid for one whole week. Finally my cousin, who knew where I was, came to find me.

"You have to come home," he said. "Your marks have been posted for six days on the school doors. All the people know that you received a Division One. Everyone is over-joyed with your success. Our two Uncles have each slaughtered a chicken to have a celebration in your honour."

"All right, I guess I can come back," I said softly. "I don't want to make my Uncles angry."

After that graduation party, I was proud of my academic accomplishments and decided to complete my academic courses before I thought about university. I opted to continue Form Five and Six to finish my O levels and then my A levels—in the manner of the British system. They had established their educational system while they controlled Kenya and after our independence in 1963 we continued on with it for a time.

The Ministry of Education had ruled that for the A levels, eighty-five percent of those students with the necessary marks could attend in the Kakamega District and fifteen percent had to go to schools outside the district. I had chosen to go to any school outside the district. I received two letter of offers to complete Form Five and Six in schools in Bugoma District.

I knew people at Kamusingu School and my teachers at home advised me to go there. Following their advice, I chose that one. I was able to go to Kamusingu by May, though classes had started in February.

Again I was sponsored by Lorrie Williams, through CHES which, by then, awarded scholarships to bright boys and girls from very needy backgrounds so that they could go to secondary school.

For the first one and a half years I did not do well at that school. It was not completely my fault because the school itself had problems. Teachers were transferred and not replaced—meaning there were no teachers for classes. We students demonstrated in front of the school. As a result, the Principal was demoted. In the final exams, I got eight points in Kiswahili and a subsidiary pass in Geography and History. With these grades I couldn't attend university. I missed the entrance requirements by only two points. I wanted to re-do the course, but couldn't because CHES would not support me repeating the year. Instead I went to a college and received a teaching diploma. Even though I had not been able to attend university through no real fault of my own, I still saw a bright future ahead.

I told my parents, "Very soon I will change our home and our lives when I have a teaching job. We will not have to borrow from our neighbours or relatives during the hunger season from March to May when we have no maize left in our house."

Life continued to look good. In 1988, at nineteen years of age, I started teaching Geography and Kiswahili, our national language, at Jubilee Secondary School in Siaya District for three months. I still lived at home, and so I had to walk the seven kilometers each way to work. I prepared and marked students' assignments from the thirty lessons I taught each week. In addition, I had to negotiate my own contract with the Board of Governors of Jubilee School. The best I could do was 1200 Shillings ($24.00 Canadian) per month. The only reason I was able to get this teaching position was that it had been unfilled for over a month, leading to a complaint by the teachers on staff.

In July, the Principal of my former high school, Hector Sutherland, approached me to come and teach at his present school, Shikunga Secondary. I was relieved when I took on that position. There were only twenty lessons of Kiswahili each week and the Board provided me with a house to live in so I didn't have a long walk to and from work. I have remained there to this day, mainly teaching Kiswahili and Geography.

In 1996, I was appointed the school counsellor. Very few counsellors were trained before they took that position. I certainly was not, but I had good relationships with the students and liked to help them solve their problems. After I was appointed I attended short courses on counselling.

I really liked my job. I still do individual guidance and counselling and teach specific life and career topics one day a week. In addition I am now a member of the District Counselling Committee and taking a diploma course in Guidance and Counselling at Kenya Polytechnic.

From my 6,000 Shillings ($120.00 Canadian) monthly salary, I support my wife, two sons and one daughter, my Father and Mother. I live on the same *shamba,* farm, that I grew up on.

I am proud to be recognized as one of the best teachers at Shikunga High School. I have received awards, certificates of merits, and trophies over the years for my service there. When I look back on my background, so immersed in poverty, I realize that, with Canadian sponsorship and my own hard work, I am a success story. Also, I am the first professional person in my family. The only other persons in our clan to have a regular pay-cheque are some uncles in the printing business. I feel proud to be a teacher because people approach me for advice or ask me to be on a committee. I am looked up to because I have been so involved in the school and the community. I play and coach at the local football club. Because I am such an athlete, I coached football, or soccer as you call it, at school. I taught the young people on the football team how to make the moves of the game and I even played with them at the matches.

My strength in music led me to train and lead the bands at Shikunga Secondary School. When I was a young person my Father taught me how to play the guitar and I went to competitions at the Music Festivals. I also learned to play the drums. I feel I have given back lots to my school community.

Also, I take care of my sister's first-born. He is such a bright boy and my sister had to get him out of the area where they live because tribal clashes were disrupting the village. My other sister died in 1998.

Since 2002, I have been trying to be hired as a Government teacher because it would be a permanent position, with a pension. I am not worried that I have to wait awhile for the type of position I want. I know I can keep my present counselling assignment and wait for a government job to open at my school. I am heartened by the rule that first priority must always be given to teachers working at the school. It seems like a safe, logical way to proceed, rather than applying to a variety of schools.

If I get a government teaching position, all of my children will have a chance to go to secondary school. I want my children to be successful in education and in life. My first born is in Standard Three, the second born is in Standard Two and our youngest, who is three years old, goes to nursery school next year. I am saying to my wife that, next year, when all three of our children are in school I want her to start a small business at a kiosk in the market. I will set it up and she can manage it.

I will continue to work hard and be committed to what I am doing. If chances come my way, I would like to continue learning through taking more courses. I can't sponsor myself right now because my money must go towards my children's school fees. To keep on learning about education, I read and attend seminars. Education is a profession that requires non-stop learning. I facilitate workshops for others and present papers to educators, some of whom have gone to university. I am in the final stages of writing a book on Guidance and Counselling. When I gave my manuscript to my former Principal to edit, he told me he would get me to do more in-service training because he thought the content was so thorough.

So life is good and I am content."

Philip Entende

Logical, assured and confident.

A family man, hardworking and content,

Proud of his accomplishments as a teacher and counsellor.

A man who embodies the belief that teachers mould the future.

PHOTO COURTESY JAY PROCKTOR

🏵 Florence Iminza

"*I* must have been very young at the time. While I don't remember my exact age, I do remember picking the low leaves off the tea plants on one of the tea estates in the Nandi Hills with my Mother and my other six brothers and sisters."

So starts our first conversation over lunch at Sheywe Guest House. In an open *banda* on the heavily treed grounds, Florence and I sit on the blue velvet seats of formal dining room chairs. The soft wind sifts through the leaves of the gum trees. Florence has taken time from her workday for a two hour lunch so that we can talk.

She is a tall, handsome woman with a strong voice. Today, her ever-changing hair style is sleekly bobbed. Her brown and white print blouse is tucked tightly into a brown tailored skirt. A matching jacket is carefully hung on the back of her chair. Her legs are crossed and she flicks her brown pumps up and down in the silky air. An aura of confidence surrounds her.

Before the waiter brings our lunch of *ugali*, chips and beef stew, Florence continues,

"The tea estate was in the Nandi Hills, those high, rolling hills north-east of Kakamega, about a ninety minute *matatu* ride from here. In my childhood days, the sun pounded heat down upon a hot land. The sun sizzled the hills hotter than I thought I could bear. But most days the afternoon rains cooled the air that covered the hills, and washed the dusty sweat from my face.

Each of the tea estates that covered the Nandi Hills was held by a company. Our estate had a large precise patchwork of tea bushes in glim-mering shades of greens. Behind the big house were the workers' small houses, a school and a medical building—all painted sparkling white.

Like the other families, our family picked the same patch of tea on the plantation in a seventeen-day rotation. Each of us wore a wicker basket with a long leather strap that we slipped over our foreheads. That strap held the basket balanced at the back of our necks. I kept my head tilted forward to hold my basket centered as I moved slowly through the rows of tea bushes. The tea bushes were planted closely together and, from a distance, the fields of tea look like a sea of solid green. When we were between the rows, only the tops of the adults' heads peeked about the bushes as the whole family picked the leaves ready to be plucked. I loved the feeling of our heads ducking up and down among the soft leaves.

My Mother had trained me how to spot the best leaves as I moved quickly through the bushes. She worked so hard to make sure all us five children picked steadily during the hot days to meet our quota.

You need to know a little bit about my family. My Mother's name is Mary. She married my Father, Joseph, in Uganda. She spoke of it as a happy marriage. They had four children and in the days before I appeared they moved to Kenya. I was born on the tea estate in the Nandi Hills, in the Rift Valley. My Father died from an accident when I was an infant. My Mother then became the second wife of a man, also called Joseph, who had children with his first wife. This arrangement was not odd to me because most of the men had more than one wife. Even as a young child, I thought my Mother was more intelligent than my stepfather. My Mother then had two more children—Agnes and Emmanuel—with her new husband. For a time her two youngest children were too small to come to the tea bushes so they were left at home. Because my Mother's life was full of struggle and hard labour as she worked in the tea fields, I was left to care for my stepsister and stepbrother when they were babies. Later, these young ones were sometimes left on their own when I had to pick the tea leaves too.

Joseph was very cruel to his five newly acquired step-children. He often hit us for minor things and beat us when he was drunk. More often than not we would flee if we heard him approaching the compound because his appearance meant kicks and strikes with his cane. The best place was to be asleep in bed, or pretend to be doing so. It was worse, depending on how much he had drunk. Because he drank *Chang'Aa* he left his sense of responsibility outside the door. Many times he was too drunk to help us pick tea. Then we had to work harder to meet our quota so we could stay on the tea plantation estate. Because we worked there, our family had good housing, free primary education and medical assistance at the estate's hospital. The fear of losing our position at the estate pushed my mother to work so hard.

However, sometimes Joseph did make money. I am not certain how, but I do know we were expected to respect him for that. Mother said we should, but I couldn't. I tried because, as a good girl, I knew I should respect my stepfather. But I couldn't because he beat the five of us so much that I never forgave him. One good thing, and the only one, is he didn't beat my Mother or his own children he had with her. My older brothers and sisters told my Mother to get out of house, move away and to get our own house. I thought my first-born siblings were right, but now I know better. A woman needs a man.

My Mother educated my four older brothers and sisters. My two brothers went into mechanical engineering and a welding course while both my sisters were trained as tailors. After they each got a job, they never came home again. It has been over sixteen years since Mom has seen them.

I began primary school on the tea plantation when I was five because it was easier for my Mother to work in the tea fields if she didn't have me along. After a couple of months in class, I realized I was smart. I always knew the answer and raised my hand when the teacher asked a question. You know that the Kenyans have a way of teaching. The teachers tell students the information and we chant pieces of it back to them when we hear the teacher's voice rise up in a certain way. I could always tell when it was time to chant because the teacher's voice went louder and slower at the end of a sentence. The teacher finished talking and then we copied notes from the blackboard. Every week or so we were tested to see how well we remembered the facts. I always studied hard for these exams.

I started to read English in Standard Two. I was a model student— quiet, studious, and eager. I got A's in all my examinations. I was the first girl to be the top of each class.

Throughout primary levels, I was hard-working at school and on the tea plantation, but I was very different at home. I would speak out when I was asked to clean-up or prepare food. I hated how hard my Mother had to work at home and at the tea factory. At eight years old, I knew I didn't want to get married. I didn't want a life like my Mother. I really believed, then, no one was better than me.

The turning point of my life happened at Primary School. A Member of Parliament, who belonged to the Catholic Church, came to my school. The Head Teacher told him about me. He came into one of my classes and asked, "What is very important in an institution like this?"

One student said, "Teachers." Another chimed in, "Buildings." And yet another pupil cried out, "Learning."

The Minister did not seem impressed with any of these answers. He looked on his right. Teachers were lined up against the wall. Then he gazed to his left, at the church sponsors in their arrow-straight formation. Then he nodded. Something tickled my mind. I raised my hand and said, "God."

"Yes," he shouted.

I was right. Just a mere Standard Eight girl. I couldn't believe it. I was simply too happy to express myself in words. I thought then that I was one of the brightest girls in the whole school.

"You are going to be a voice to represent women," he said to me.

Because he liked my cleverness and leadership, this M.P. paid the fees for my first year of secondary school at Musudu, in the Rift Valley. Unfortunately, he withdrew his support for my second year, but my Head Master made sure I got a government bursary. My Mother worked hard to support some of my school fees. At that time she moved to her own *shamba*, farm, in a reserve area near Musudu Secondary School, in Nandi. My stepfather stayed at the tea estate.

After high school, I wanted to become a career woman, not a housewife. I wanted to do something different with my life. I wanted to help women who were suffering and to be a voice for women. I wanted women to be appreciated. Women have little power in Kenya. We are still a possession of our husband and are expected to run the house and look after the children as well as work at some type of job—if we were fortunate enough to get some education. For change to affect women, more girls must go to school and learn that as a group we want changes in our society.

In my own family, I saw my sisters follow that traditional role. My older sister is a housewife. My step-sister got married at fourteen and my youngest step-sister married young also. She now works so hard, just like my Mother did, to make money to support her two young children and a drunken husband.

I was lucky. I got an A.C.C.E.S. scholarship and went to Imara Commercial College to study accounting and computers for three years. There were two ladies and twelve men in my class. I had always loved Math in secondary school so I enjoyed Accounting. It interested and challenged me. The men believed that women could not do Math. I felt exhilarated when I beat the men in solving equations and problems in class. However, they always loved to point out my mistakes, when I made them. While I went to college I stayed with Elizabeth, a

Soroptomist in Kakamega. The Kakamega Soroptomist Club, which is a women-only offspring of the Rotary Club, also helped me with my fees and other expenses. Terry, Winnie, Frieda and Rose, all business ladies and Soroptomists in town, really affected my life.

I left college at the end of my three years and took a job as a clerk in the accounting department at the Golf Hotel in Kakamega. I was delighted to be independent and have my own money. I rented my own room in Kakamega. I bought myself clothes and shoes from the market stalls. I had my hair done regularly. I had my nails painted. I constructed a home on the *shamba* for my Mother because her old house let in the water everyday it rained. I was not pleased when my stepfather moved in with her again, but they seemed to have something in common that they still shared. He appeared to drink less now. I believed I could sacrifice for her because she had worked so hard all her life and had helped me go to school.

I left the Golf Hotel after two years to take a part-time Accounting job at A.C.C.E.S. There I learned to do accounts and to use the computer. People were so helpful to me. I stayed about a year in this job and I enjoyed meeting all the Canadians who came to A.C.C.E.S. in Kenya. I also really enjoyed getting involved with C.A.A.A., the Canadian-African Alumni Association for the graduates, as the treasurer and on the Finance Committee.

I grew tired, though, after nearly three year of working with numbers, accounts and sitting in front of the computer all day. I decided on a career change—I would work with people. I wanted to reach women who are suffering and to do more than collect a pay-cheque. I knew that I could do something else and I wanted to do more in society. Luckily, one of the A.C.C.E.S. donors decided to fund my education and she paid all my fees so I could become a pastor.

I was delighted to be accepted for a diploma in theology by the Kaimosi Friends Theological College, outside Kakamega, on the way to Nandi Hills. I belong to the Anglican Church, but I had only sufficient funds to pay for the courses at this Quaker College. I love being a student again now. I attend classes five days a week with young and old men and women. Each day we have to observe an hour of silence. At first, it was an adjustment because I had to wear simple, dark clothes and very plain, sturdy shoes. I so missed my fancy clothes and exciting shoes. I also had to get used to the food they served—very plain, small portions of basic food. I found the restrictions placed on students and the requirement that each student had to do work-study, which was a fancy word for helping to maintain the College's house and farm, to be very irritating. But eventually, I accepted all the changes.

The one thing I did insist upon was, on Sundays, I would go to my Anglican Church for the main service. I want to be a minister in the Anglican Church, but the authorities tell me they require that the minister be married. I don't want to be married. I have four years at theological college to update myself so I will work on that challenge later. It is perfect right now to be working towards something. Everyday should be better, I believe. I am trying to be positive and less of a perfectionist. I know I have the qualities of a leader. I am gaining more knowledge so I can work hand-in-hand with the gifts I know I have already.

Starting when I worked at A.C.C.E.S., I took on the treasurer position for the C.A.A.A.'s Finance Committee. I am also the treasurer of the young women's group, World of Women, at CHES. At the Friends Theological College I belong to the Young Women's Association and I am the secretary on the executive of the College.

When I finish theological college, I intend to assist others, particularly women. I have the knowledge to give counseling and guidance. I am able to comfort and motivate those people who are suffering. I will start in this area of Kakamega and then go out from here—anywhere in the world. I know the prophet is not recognized by her own people so I must go far away to do my service. I will do it. I want to make a difference."

Florence Iminza

A feminist, committed to making a difference for women,

Works to understand the past.

Strong, articulate and passionate to spread the word of the gospel.

Desiring to leave the past behind,

Anticipating the power of being a pastor.

Her future dreams are integral to the present moment.

◈ *Cappitus Chironga*

$\mathcal{A}$ young Kenyan man in navy dress pants and a white shirt strode towards where I was sitting by the large, crystal-clear swimming pool at the Fairview Hotel in Nairobi. There was a sense of pride in his bearing. We introduced ourselves and conversed about everyday matters. As a 29-year old economist with the Central Bank of Kenya, Cappitus' opening remarks revealed self-assurance tinged with humbleness and realism. He was agreeable to sitting in the warmth of the African sun while telling me his story. Cappitus talked honestly and in great depth about a life filled with hurdles and marked with amazing successes.

"According to my Mother, I was born on Thursday, June 28, 1974, at 2:00 p.m.. A lucky day, I believe. My Father and Mother had a two-acre plot of very poor soil with a one room, grass-thatched hut in Kakamega District. I am the second-born of eight children, four boys and four girls. Our family had a serious problem because my Grandfather had two wives. Grandfather's first wife had fourteen children, but only two survived—my Father and his sister, my Aunt Gladys. May she rest in peace. Like many polygamous families, there was much jealously between Grandfather's two wives. I wasn't worried about it as a child. I accepted polygamy which is legal and still widely practiced in Kenya. A man's status is raised in his tribe if he takes more than one wife. In a rural district, like Kakamega, the majority of the men in the Luyha tribe practice that tradition.

My Father was bright, but he never went too far in school, so getting a job and providing for his children was difficult. He just worked on others' farms to get some cash for our upkeep.

I went to school, but in Standard Three I dropped out to become a cattle herder to earn money to buy myself school uniforms and books. I earned 3500 Shillings (about $58.00 Canadian) each month. However, my plan did not work, as the money was used to purchase basic food for our family and treatment of my eldest sister who had developed breast cancer. From my salary, I saved 50 Shillings, less than $1.00 Canadian, for my schooling. In 1986, I went back to school and was placed in Standard

Five. I never attended Standard Four. I guess the teachers must have recognized my persistence and a glimmer of intelligence.

I remember studying very early each morning before I went to school. At the end of the second term I held the third place in academic standing, and by the end of the final term I was in the number one spot.

My memory of that time centers on my desire and anticipation of going to school. I loved school. Once I began attending, a new pattern of living emerged for me. I rose at 5:00 a.m. and read by the light of a tin lamp fed by paraffin. I left at 6:00 and walked barefoot for three kilometres to school. Then I read my textbooks until school began at 8:30. Classes and clean-up finished by 5:00 p.m., but I stayed in the classroom to study and read until 6:30. Then I walked home. After the morning activities on Saturday, I took my books to school in the afternoon so I could read in the quietness of the classroom.

I maintained first position in all my examinations to Standard Eight and was ready for secondary school in 1989. After primary school, I had no money to pay the school fees. In those days I never knew what the future might hold. I was so worried about my prospects.

My cousin's family included a pharmacist, nurse and teacher. I thought they would help me with money to continue at secondary education, but they wouldn't. At that point, I just gave up and became resigned to being a peasant farmer like my Mother. Using a hand hoe, I used to report to work on our farm at 5:30 a.m. and finish for the day at 11:00. My aim was to reduce the food shortage that had become a permanent feature since my birth. Because of this hard work, coupled with hunger, my figure became like that of a very old man. I worked like this in the fields for a period of six months. I was discouraged and frustrated. I thought I should just get some type of job and plan to be like the others in my community and get married when I was eighteen. I couldn't see any future for myself.

In February 1990, my Mother had her last-born—a boy called Sammy. After Sammy's birth, my Father took the bus to Nairobi to talk to those cousins who had refused us before. He was successful in persuading one of them, the pharmacist, to give him 4,500 Shillings ($75.00 Canadian dollars) towards my school fees for St. Mary's Secondary School where I had been assigned a place. This donation of my cousin would help me, but I still fell short of what I needed to attend school.

I have found life has its own way of unfolding. Unpredictable things occur which open the door to new opportunities. On the 7th of February, I was strolling in the Musalaba Market, our local shopping area, and randomly sat by a disabled cobbler. While I was talking to this poor man, a elderly white lady came by with a shoe to repair. She spoke only English and I could speak a little English too. She slowly explained to me how she wanted her shoe repaired. I repeated her directions, in Luyha, to the cobbler. While her shoe was being repaired, she asked why I was not in school. I explained to her I did not have enough money to continue with my secondary school education. She told me that her name was Ann and she was an Agent for CHES. She said she would like me to visit her office at Ekambuli Secondary School. The next week I made the journey to this school. After that meeting, she realized how very poor and needy I was and said she would sponsor me for the rest of my secondary school education.

Later Ann and I took a *matatu*, a decrepit mini-bus, to Kisumu and bought all the supplies and clothes I needed for school. Ann bought my first blanket. Before then, I had only a sugar sack to sleep in.

However, my place at St. Mary's School was already taken because I had been late in registering. My Father and I went to Kakamega Secondary School on February 28th to see whether they had an opening. They did. I became the only student from my village of 200,000 people to attend such a prestigious secondary school. Ann supported me all through secondary school. In her gift of a scholarship to me, she opened my life to a new world. Her simple act of giving changed me forever.

At Kakamega Secondary School, life was at its best. I loved learning. I made friends with young people, eager like me to learn. Many were from other communities and from Asian families. I had never before had an opportunity to meet and associate with the Asian students whose fathers ran most of the businesses in Kakamega town. My Physics teacher, Franklin Ahura, and the Chemistry teacher, Rose Munyendo, were also very good to me. They told me they saw something special in me.

In Form Two, as a Perfect of the Social Buildings and an official in the Agricultural Club, I joined other students to do many projects. We grew and sold vegetables in our school throughout my entire secondary school years. By growing some vegetables myself and selling them to the school kitchen, I made a little money for my personal needs. The only money my family contributed was the 4,500 Shillings my Father had given me in Form One. In reality, I always had the feeling I was without enough money.

In Form Three, I was appointed Secretary of the Agricultural Club. This was a real honour. In addition, I prepared a science exhibit in Physics that I took to a competition at the national level. The topic was: Using Solar Energy to Warm Up Water, using polythene paper and reflective materials. I demonstrated how that could be done. My Chemistry exhibition also went to the provincial levels. In this science project I used salt to preserve vegetables. I actually boiled them in salt, which preserved their chlorophyll level.

At that time, I had carefully looked at all the universities and colleges' course outlines and, in the end, selected a degree in electrical engineering. At the end of Form Four, I graduated—but not in the top student category. I had scored 40/48—rather than the forty-two required for the entrance into electrical engineering. I couldn't believe the results.

I was called to the university to pursue a Bachelor of Arts degree. At first I did not like the course, as that degree was not considered marketable. This perception was based on lack of information. What really gave a lot of encouragement was reading about the life of the Kenya's third President; His Excellency Emilio Mwai Kibaki. I read about his academic and professional prowess. He graduated with a First Class honours in Economics from Makerere University in Uganda and with Distinction at the Masters level from London School of Economics. He became my role model because during his tenure as the Minister for Finance Kenya sustained high growth levels. I decided that I wanted to be like him. I resolved to take this university offer of a Bachelor of Arts and then try to get into a major in Economics.

At the University of Nairobi, I knew a student could apply to change programmes in the first month of classes. If there was space, normally a student was placed in his preference. At that time the Economics department did not have many students wanting to be Economists. I guess most of the rural students didn't think an Economics degree would lead to a job. But, I knew it had worked for our then Vice-President Kibaki, and so I believed it would do the same for me.

Upon receiving my admission letter, the support from the A.C.C.E.S. Scholarship fund came in. That money was a life-line. The scholarship took care of all my fees during the four years as an undergraduate to supplement the government loans. That meant that I did not have financial stress at the university. I would not have completed this course without A.C.C.E.S.' assistance.

On November 25, 1995, my life as an under-graduate began. I

registered for a Bachelor of Arts, a degree specializing in Economics, Mathematics and Geography. I knew I had to excel and be one of the top students in my class. Also, from my reading and personal analysis, I understood that I should be active in the Economic Clubs at the university. In addition to the clubs, I attended special presentations, workshops and even joined professional associations outside the university.

In 1996, my dream came true. I became the Organizing Secretary of the Economics Students Association. The club had been inactive, a bit dead you might say, but as the organizing secretary the following year, I marketed the club to public and corporate bodies. They developed great interest, so much so that the club revived and, during 1997 and 1998, it was THE club to join. Up to 1999, our Club did so much and the members got the opportunity to know so many C.E.O.'s and executives of senior companies.

The companies began to recruit for new employees through our Economics Club. My involvement in making a success of this Economics Club helped me realize I did have a future—a future that involved a good position in the business, banking or the government sectors.

At the end of the second year I was in the overall third top position of student achievement. I was given the opportunity of selecting just one focus. Of course, I took Economics for the third and fourth years. I wanted to be in the top class. I graduated with first class in Economics. On the 48 units of my programme, I had 45 A's.

In addition to being a very disciplined person at university, I was respected as a strong member of the Catholic Church. My respect and belief in God guided me into active membership in my church's activities. I was also a close friend to our church priest. Our university Chaplain, Father Thomas MacDonald—a priest from Ireland, became my close friend.

One day Father Tom called me into his office and asked me to sit down. "Cappitus, after graduation, don't go back to your village and sit there. Stay in Nairobi and see what you can do here."

I was surprised. I only knew I wanted a job—anywhere. Because of his advice, I decided to seek a job in the city. I was trusted enough to be a worker in the rehabilitation of the street children in Nairobi. I worked with the children's organization, called Childlife Trust, until March 2000.

In January 2000, Father Tom advised me to apply for a scholarship for my Masters in Economics.

"But I am from a poor extended family," I responded. "My elder sister dropped out of school and married in 1990. My brother and sister are not able to proceed with secondary school education. I have a younger sister and brother who have been at home for a full year because my parents can't afford to pay their fees. I also want my brothers and sisters to study. If you tell me to go to school rather than get a job, how will it look if I have everything? They have nothing. I want them to go back to school."

"I understand the problems of Africa," the Priest replied. "I have been here for more than 20 years. I really do know. But there is a scholarship for Catholic students available from Germany. And there are scholarships for the Masters' programme offered by the University of Nairobi. You are very bright and ambitious. Apply for both and see where it takes you."

I took his advice and applied for both scholarships. In March 2000, I received a letter from Germany that I had been awarded the Catholic Academic Exchange Programme Scholarship to study at the University of Nairobi. A few months later, in July, I also received a scholarship from the University of Nairobi. After considering the two offers, I chose the Catholic Scholarship because it was more substantial and could help me assist my family. Sometime in August 2000, I started my classes for my Masters.

Just after I settled on the scholarship, however, I saw in our newspaper, The Daily Nation, an advertisement for a position in the Management Trainees Programme at the Central Bank of Kenya. I knew this was a definite opportunity that might not open up again for a long while. I was in a dilemma about what I should do. With the German scholarship I had decided I would use some for myself and give some to my brothers and sisters' education. I was focused now on pursuing further studies, but this opportunity of training for a job with the Central Bank caused me to analyze the situation. After careful consideration, I applied for the Management Trainees Programme at the Central Bank.

On July 31, 2000 I went for the first interviews with the Central Bank of Kenya—along with three hundred and fifty other applicants. There were so many of us I thought that I wouldn't stand a chance. As I waited for my interview, I talked to some of the others and found that they had Master degrees from other universities. I didn't think I had a hope.

After two weeks, I was called in for a second interview. Shortly afterwards, I found I had passed this round and would be among seventy-five people to be considered for the training programme. At that point I called Father Tom to talk over my situation. In early September, I went in for the interview and found I was one of the six candidates selected for the third round of interviews. That took place on October 15 or 18. I can't recall the date very well because my head was in such a spin in those days. After the interview, everything went quiet.

Around November 20th, I received a letter from the Central Bank to go for medical tests, which included a blood test for HIV. From this letter, I knew I had the job. Now, I faced a major problem. I had committed myself to a scholarship and was about to finish my first semester at university. And there was a job coming at the Central Bank of Kenya. Should I quit my studies and take the position was a question that rocketed back and forth in my mind.

Again, I went back to Father Tom. "I don't want to hurt you, Father," I said. "You gave me a way to get a scholarship. But there is this job opportunity and I have a poor family. They are looking to me for help."

"You must write a letter to your sponsors and explain your family background," Father Tom replied. "Tell them you must leave your studies because you have a job. But you would appreciate enough money to cover the tuition as a part-time student. You know the University of Nairobi has just introduced a Parallel Programme."

"What type of programme is that?"

"A new one. You can work during the day time and take courses in the evenings and on Saturdays. You will have to forget about everything else if you pursue this line."

I wrote to my sponsors in Germany, telling them just what Father told me. They gave me my tuition costs. In January 2001, I started working for the Central Bank of Kenya in their training program. It was an extremely hard schedule. I slept for only four hours a night. The Bank required that I go to all the departments and all the branches, including Kisumu and Mombasa, during the two years. I also had to write individual reports and present them to management on how things could be improved in the Bank.

This was at the same time as I was doing the course work for my M.A. in Arts and Economics, and doubling as the Education Secretary of Catholic Association of Students in East Africa. At the University of Nairobi I had to write exams every three months. It was a tough road to walk, but I made it.

I finished my Management Trainee Programme with the Central Bank in May 2002. Upon completion, I was posted in the Financial

Markets Department and National Debt Division. The government at that time was concerned with the national debt structure. Most of the money was in Treasury Bills and one third was in bonds. My boss wanted me to come up with a proper bond-pricing programme. I was very nervous because it was to be a public programme. I had to design the types of bonds and how to market them. I went for two weeks in the Bank's Library and learned all about bonds, using Internet browsing as part of my research. Within a month, I had designed a pricing strategy, a marketing strategy and an audition strategy for bonds.

In July 2002, we launched the debt-restructuring programme with Auction Bonds. Just over a year later Treasury Bonds dominated the debt market. I was proud of the work I did. What I did touched the entire economy of Kenya.

I finished my Master in 2003 and graduated in May 2004, due to lecturers' strike, with A's and B's. I was admitted to the University of Warwick for my Masters in Financial Economics because I wanted to have diversity in my career. I went for an interview at the British Embassy in December 2003, after which about six of us were each awarded a scholarship. Warwick has also offered me a bursary to cover twenty percent of my expenditures during my stay in London. The programme will take one year, finishing in September 2005.

During this time I married my wife, Mary who is a lecturer at the Oshwal College and projects analyst with Kenyan Programme for Disabled Persons. She has a Masters of Business Administration in Human Resources. We have two sons, Thomas Ryan, 2 years old and Augustine, 5 months. I named our first born Thomas, after Father Tom MacDonald because he helped me so much. I know I want to give my son what I didn't have.

The most important virtue in my life is that I haven't forgotten my roots or my family. I don't like to see family or friends in problems when I can help. I built a house for my parents in our village. I want to build them a better one when I can. I give them money for food and medicine. I paid my sister's fees to get a housekeeping and laundry certificate at Kenya Utalii College. Going to that type of trades' college costs far more than the fees for university. I have paid my younger brother's school fees and expenses through secondary school. He has now finished Form Four and is waiting to join college. My younger sister, Gladys went to Shikunga Boarding School in 2001. She is now the head girl in Form Three. Next year, most of my brothers and sisters will be through their basic secondary education. Only two children are still in primary school. I hope to be able to pay their way through secondary school. In addition, I now look after one of the children of my Aunt. Her husband died of HIV and she died just last July. She approached me before she passed away to see if I would educate one of her daughters, Everlyne. Everlyne is now in Form Three. I may also pay for her brother if I can. I have ensured that a younger brother of a close friend of mine who died of AIDS has funds to complete his secondary education. I pay for so many young people's education that I want to set up a Foundation or to be a partner in one. This Foundation would pay for children's fees and expenses so that they can go to school.

As I look back in life, I easily understand that my Mother, Teresah Ayuma, plays a very important role in my life. She endured a lot. She has always been so very patient. Everyday she used to check our school-books. She is honest and disciplined and works very hard. She used to pray a lot for us. I really admire her faith and life of simplicity. She is a great woman. I will always try to ensure her comfort.

I am really thankful I met the CHES Agent, Ann, who made me know that there was a way out of my poverty. A.C.C.E.S. kept the door open by providing the scholarship for my university. The high standards expected by both CHES and A.C.C.E.S. trained me well. I am one of the very few well-paid graduates in Kenya.

I have a good life. People have assisted me along the way and that is why I want to help my brothers, sisters, cousins and friends through school. It is only through education that our people will see change in their lives.

I look back in my life and see a lot of blessings. Upon return from Britain, I want to give more to charity. God Bless CHES! God bless A.C.C.E.S.! God bless all those who shaped and touched my life. Without you, I would not be there to tell this story."

Cappitus Chironga

A man with a strong faith in himself and in God

Is on a journey to the top.

Brilliant mind, analytical, and patient,

He moves swiftly toward a position of power.

Hard-working, determined, and self-disciplined

Bank Accountant who is now completing his second Masters.

Driven to help others.

A man with the future of Kenya on his shoulders.

PHOTO COURTESY JAY PROCKTOR

▨ *Margaret Mmbone*

Polytechnic Clinic,
Kisumu, Kenya

January 12

Dear Sandra,

No doubt, you'll be surprised to receive this letter. When I talked to you last month at Rose's Dress shop about joining the Soroptomist Club in Kakamega, I understood you wanted some background information about my life. So now, I am putting pen to paper. In my letter, you will read of a woman's life that is somewhat similar to, and yet most different from, your own.

I am now thirty, the oldest of four children in my family and the first-born female. I come from a single parent family. No, that is not quite right. My Mother and Father separated when I was seven, but I was never told the reason for their splitting up. My Mother took the four of us to live in her mother's house in Masoli. Two of my Mother's brothers were still living in my Grandmother's house. Mom stayed for only a short while, and then she left to find work in Nairobi. Or that's what she said. She rarely came back to see us. Without telephones or money for postage, the only way to contact us was in person. She came back on occasion, but the visits became less after she married again and had two other children.

Even though Grandmother had not gone to school, she had made sure my Mother did. My Mother completed primary school, but dropped out of secondary school to work and then marry my Father. When I was six, my Grandmother decided I was to go to school. She repeatedly said girls should be educated. I knew she was saying something different from what the community believed because most girls I knew did not get a chance to go to school. If the family had any money for school fees, then the boys were educated. My Grandmother stood by her belief because she paid the fees for my entire primary school years. I helped her by working in the farmers' fields to make money to pay for my school uniforms and books.

As the oldest girl in the house, I was expected to do all the domestic jobs. Starting at 5:30 a.m. and finishing about ten at night. In the darkness before dawn, my first responsibility was gathering wood and making the fire under the black metal *jiko,* a pot with three short legs. I filled this large pot with water and placed it over burning charcoal. As it was heating up to a boil, I ran to the river with a bucket to bring the day's water and fill the large clay water-storage pot in the corner of the cooking room. Then I made the maize porridge, *uji,* and served metal bowls of it to the family. Only then did I have a few minutes to clean-up and wash my cotton dress for the next day. You didn't know me then, but I had only two cotton dresses. One to wear while the other one was washed and hung on the bushes to dry. After all my chores were done, I ran off to primary school. I always tried to get to school on time and most days I was successful.

I ran home at lunch to prepare a meal for my younger brothers, my Uncles, and Grandmother. I prepared *ugali*—a cornmeal mixture cooked in water and then beaten until thick and smooth. When we had bananas on our trees outside, I would cut up some of them. Then we children dashed back to school.

At the end of the school day the female students had to do the women's work at school—sweep the dirt floors, put away books in the storage trunks, and wipe off the desks. The boys were able to play games or study. When I returned home, I usually had to go for more water from the river. On the way home I looked for vegetables in the field. On some days I would go to the mill to get the maize ground into flour and drop into the market to get some grains or *sukuma,* a green-leafed vegetable that tastes something like bitter kale. When I returned, I ran out to the ditches and fields to collect a few pieces of firewood. After piling the branches beside our hut, I hurried into the cooking room to fix *ugali* and *sukuma wiki,* which is boiled *sukuma,* but slippery in texture, for our supper. By the time we sat down to eat it was often 9:30 p.m. After I washed the dishes, I settled by the table to do my homework. The nights we had no paraffin for our lamp, I would go immediately to bed. I was so tired. When the full moon hung large and bright in the dark heavens, I remember reading and doing my school assignments by its light.

On the weekends, the four of us worked in the fields or took care of the cattle. Every day of the week had the same routine. The only change was on the occasional days when I couldn't get all my jobs in the house done. Because I had neglected my duties, I couldn't go to school and I was beaten by my Uncle or my Grandmother. As you know, this is life for the hundreds of thousands of Luyha women in Western Province.

I had such feelings of frustration from being overworked. It was so rare in a Kenyan family that a child spoke about her feelings, but I became so angry that I blurted out something about the way I felt to my Grandmother.

"I don't know why I have to do all the work for everyone else in this family. It's not fair," I stated. "The boys and my sister should have to help me."

"You have no right to say this," my Grandmother shouted at me, as she hit me with a stick over and over on my shoulders. "Get the wood now. I don't want to hear one more word."

I would remain quiet until the frustration built up in me again. Sometimes I remembered what my Grandmother had repeatedly told me about her life. She had never gone to school. Her Father had told her to stay at home and take care of the banana plantation, while the boys went to school to learn to read. Though she never went to school, I knew she was smart, a very intelligent woman. She was bright and strong, but not smart enough to break out of the Kenyan customs that women had to do all the work and a beating would correct and control children's behaviour. I can understand now how she must have felt at that time. Her daughter had dropped off her own four children and then disappeared to Nairobi. My Grandmother was left to support us. My two Uncles hung around home, like little kings, until after the four of us left when we were in our teens. During the time when we were in primary school, two of her daughters arrived with their children to seek financial support and a place to live in the hut. Just imagine the crowd of people swarming in my Grandmother's three-roomed *banda*. One thing I remember was that Grandmother kept one room as her own bedroom and her own territory. The rest of us had to use the floor in the sitting room to sleep on.

In Standard One, my brother, Francis, was also sent to school—even though he was only six. I think Grandmother sent him with me to get him out of the house. He was always questioning and challenging her and my Uncles, and that made her angry. Francis was treated worse than I was, and suffered so many beatings.

Because Francis was placed in the same class as I was, I competed with him on every assignment and on every test. He was smart and hard-working, like me. I think being in daily competition with him developed my attitude that I must be better, more successful, than a man. Before primary school I had hated all the work I had to do to take care of the family. I resented that this was a female's role in life. For the first time, at school, I realized, on the level playing field of academics, I could achieve more than a male. I was so proud and driven by my successes to do even better. In Standard Eight, I was the first pupil at Busilwa Primary school to achieve 58 out of a total of 60 marks. I was called to be a student at several secondary schools because of my high marks. My Grandmother was very proud of me. She kept telling me every day she was so pleased with my success at school. I even heard her bragging to my Aunts and Uncles and neighbours about my success. It was as if some of my accomplishments were a reflection of her.

However, things looked dark after primary school as my Grandmother had no money for the secondary school fees. My Mother came home from Nairobi and wanted me to work as a maid.

In unison, Grandmother and I said "No" to that idea. Then my Grandmother said something to my Mother that surprised me.

"I am not educated. I never had a job to make money and better my lot. I made sure you went to school—right up until you dropped out of secondary school to marry that man. Although he was a business man, you ran away from him and back to me with your four children. Then you left your own flesh and blood with me when you went to Nairobi to look for a job. Did you get one? All you got was another husband and more children. Now you come back and tell your daughter to leave her schooling and be a maid. Have you no hope for the future? You just want the past to come around again and again. Women's lives will never change until girls are educated enough to go to university or college. If we want change in our life we must strive for it and never give up hope. Go back to your own house in Nairobi and stay there. You are not wanted here."

My Mother left immediately. But Grandmother never gave up hope that I would continue on at school. I remember her, one evening, calling to me.

"Sit here with me by the fire," she said. I joined her.

"We will keep on trying to get some money to send you to school. A distant cousin of mine talked to me today. There are some sponsors from Canada who provide money for fees at Imbale Secondary School. I am going there tomorrow. Luck will come. You will see. The thing is to never, ever, give up on your hope."

The next day, my Grandmother walked to Imbale Secondary School and she talked with the Head Master. He introduced my Grandmother to a Canadian woman from CHES, who was in the school. Grandmother told her my story.

"The chances for this term are over. All the scholarships have been awarded," the Agent explained. "I will ask the Head Master to enroll her. If she continues to work hard and gets top marks, she might have a chance to get a scholarship next term."

My Grandmother walked the long distance home in a daze. She was so happy that luck had arrived. When she arrived home she called me from the *jiko* where I was cooking *ugali* for supper.

"Your luck has turned to gold. All you have to do is go to Imbale Secondary School and achieve high marks," she said. "I know you can because that's all you've done in primary school. You were the best in the class every year."

The next day, I attended school. I walked from my Grandmother's *shamba* in Masoli to Imbali Secondary School. It is a long time to walk twice a day, but I did it. Everyday I tried my best to learn all that I needed to know. Every night, after I did all the chores, I studied, read and made notes by the light of a paraffin lamp. I worked on the weekends for money to buy paraffin and soap. I did well and was placed in the top of the Form. The Agent at CHES was so pleased that she arranged the scholarship for the next term.

Francis came to Imbali Secondary School the year after I started. Grandmother had told him that after Standard Eight he had to go to work to make money because she had to pay for her own two sons' education. My Grandmother didn't have enough funds to pay for four secondary fees. After that Francis gave up hope for a short while and did poorly on his final examinations. He had to repeat Standard Eight while I went on to the secondary school. However, he was persistent and came to Imbale on a CHES scholarship the next year.

While I was in Form Two, CHES organized for all their girls on a secondary school scholarship at Imbale to live at a nearby compound. They wanted to see if our academic performance would improve if we ate and studied there. We had more time to study because we didn't have to walk the long distance to and from school and we didn't have all the domestic chores to do. We got to go home on the weekends. I saw that

Grandmother did all the house chores during the week while I was gone. None of the boys had to do them. At that time, Francis went to live with my Mother who had moved to Kakamega with her two children.

I continued at school until part way through Form Three, like your Grade Eleven. Then my Father reappeared in my life. No one had known where he was before, but I was so happy to see him. I had wanted to see him again for so many years. However, the Father I met now was bitter. He had married again, but that relationship was deteriorating although they had two children. He wanted the four of us kids to be with him. We visited him at his house in Nairobi. My stepmother didn't want us there, so our chance to be with our Father stopped.

That changed. After I completed my fourth Form I stayed with my Father. My two youngest brothers came to visit at holidays. I don't know what I felt during this time of change. A mixture of bitterness and rejection.

I guess my competition with the boys never faltered during secondary school. I had to prove to myself that I could do as well or better than they could. All through secondary school I had competed with the boys and continued to achieve well. My school-leaving mark was C+. It was extremely rare for a girl to get an A or B because so much of her time out of school was gobbled up with doing the traditional women's work. We got to study only when every chore was done. Often we were just too exhausted to open our books.

All through secondary school I wanted to be a nurse. I talked with Father Pat O'Connell, our parish priest in Musoli. He was my friend. I told him I wanted to do something in the nursing field. He suggested I volunteer at the clinic at Musoli and that he would talk to the Matron on my behalf. The Matron, who was a nun, was happy to have me volunteer. When she transferred to Kisii, a town south of Kisumu, she took me along. At that time I made applications to two Nursing Schools. One was in Nairobi and the other in Mukumu. The wait between secondary school and college was such a long time that I became somewhat discouraged.

Finally, I was accepted into Mukumu Nursing School. I got a faster response because Father Pat knew the Principal. It was such a surprise for me because I wasn't a Catholic then. A.C.C.E.S. granted me a scholarship for my three years of courses. I was so delighted! I was on my way to reaching my dream.

When I joined the nursing college, I knew life was changing. Nursing school was challenging. Each nurse-in-training had to work on probation in a ward for nine months, followed by three months of classes and then three months of practicum in the wards. The emphasis was on respecting others, discipline and working hard. I think it sometimes made the nursing trainees discouraged. There was really a powerful hierarchy in the school. If a student nurse made one mistake, she was sent back six months, or suspended, or expelled. It was very challenging and sometimes I think they abused us emotionally. However, Mukumu has a strong reputation for producing good nurses. From my training, I think that is true. I felt very well trained when I finished in 1998.

Once I finished my nurses' training, I got a position, in Kisumu, at the Polytechnic Clinic—working with day patients. For the first time I started making my own money and assisted with the school fees of my younger brother and sister. I also gave money to my Grandmother who was in her seventies, and to my Mother who had re-married and moved to Kakamega District. Unfortunately, her husband was a problem. I looked at the example of my Mother and I saw how she was hampered by lack of training in a specific occupation as well as by her choices in life.

My life was really good and made better by the fact I was engaged after graduation. I had met Poli in Kisii when I was volunteering with the Matron at the clinic. He liked me right from the start and he wrote to me at the nursing school. I certainly answered his letters because I liked him very much. Poli even made some visits to see me at the school. I thought Poli was a good man and so we got married in July 1999. I decided to marry because I wanted someone to love and to love me and with whom I could share my problems. My husband is a Social Studies teacher and has his Counselling Diploma. He wants to do his Masters, too. I also want to go back to school for higher studies—to get my Bachelor of Science in Nursing. I like the way my husband and I are professionals together.

When I look back on my life I realize I was aggressive. I really had a "Go for it" attitude. Something inside me urged me to try harder. I remember visualizing myself somewhere else, other than living in the *banda* and working on my Grandmother's farm. I can remember my Grandmother telling me, "You can do it!" countless times whenever I set out to do something new or complained about my present way of life. I guess my Grandmother's attitude that you never gave up on your hope to reach your goals rubbed off on me.

Giving monetary support to my family has financially strapped me. I have not yet been able to get a really stable, well-paid job. I want to go back to school to get my Bachelor of Nursing so I can become a consultant. Life is dragging at the moment, but I know this time is just another hurdle to get over. I can manage that. I believe I can open doors for other women. I talk to women and to the students at the Nursing College, encouraging them to work hard. Women must not think they're inferior. I tell them they can be on their own and be self sufficient. They mustn't depend on men because most of our men here are not reliable. I share with them I only gained respect from my husband when I got my own job.

I believe education will make a difference to the role of women. Now, women are just a piece of property to work hard for the men. But, as individual women make strides ahead to change their lives, step-by-step change will happen for more women.

My own goal is to work with women and children, particularly orphans. That is why I am so excited about being part of the Soroptomist Club because I know the outstanding work they do to make a difference in women's life. Women working together for change will make a difference. I say, "Go for it Women. You can do it, only if you work hard. Like my Grandmother."

My Warmest Regards,
Margaret.

Margaret Mmbone

A nurse committed to change for women.

Hard-working, confident and proud,

Truly believes education will make a difference in Kenya.

A living example of her beliefs.

A true feminist dedicated to helping other women.

Margaret trained at the Nursing School at Mukumu Hospital, just outside Kakamega. Here is a Mother with her day-old infant.

✺ *Godfrey Musila*

*H*is face charged with excitement, Godfrey strolled into the A.C.C.E.S. office. Godfrey was a person whose intellect emerged as he spoke. From all our previous meetings I had known him to be a quiet, handsome man who listened carefully before he responded. I observed how his dark brown eyes intently examined me as we conversed. His responses were soft-spoken, in a level tone of voice, but indicated thoughtfulness and intelligence. He was a young man, 26 years old, who talked little, but accomplished much.

Godfrey was the chairperson of the student alumni at A.C.C.E.S. He had just arrived from a nine-hour bus ride over tattered highways from Nairobi. I was to interview him about his background, but his face told me he had something important to share with me first.

Godfrey came over to me and we shook hands.

"Good afternoon, Sandra. I hope things are going well with you," he said, following the Kenyan emphasis on greetings. "I have something very important to share with you. I was awarded a scholarship for a Masters Degree at the Centre for Human Rights at the University of Pretoria, in South Africa."

"Godfrey, such wonderful news."

"Only thirty top students from across Africa were placed out of two hundred forty applications. I am extremely excited about this. It is like my dreams are coming true. It will launch me, hopefully, into an international career, but I still want to be of use to my country."

"What an honour for you and your family. When do you go?"

"Next month. We students will spend six months at Pretoria University and then split into groups to go to affiliate universities after the first semester," he said in a rush of words. "I will be going to the Universidade Eduardo Mondlane, in Maputo, Mozambique for my second semester at the beginning of July, 2004. I chose to go there because I am currently learning Portuguese and this will be a good chance to practice it. There are many uncertainties, but I guess adventure is part of the game! What is important is that this one year Master's programme is geared towards training young human rights lawyers and scholars for the future."

"Well, Godfrey, what an accomplishment to start our interview with. Can I offer you a tea and then you can talk about your childhood and your life and dreams as a student. Describe your life leading up to this present accomplishment."

"That's easy to do. I was born in Kakamega. My family was, in many respects, different from most Luyhas. My Father had only one wife, my Mother. She had a small business that sold cloth to support our family. My Father did odd jobs until 1980 when he became a pastor. My family was modest, but religious. We had the values of hard work, perseverance and hope about the future instilled in us from our parents.

We had to move back to our rural home when the family business, which was doing relatively well by the standards of the mid-1980's, ran aground. I was pretty young and did not understand much, but I gathered the move was a turning point in our lives. Mother wouldn't talk about the reason for the move later when I wanted to know more about it. I am convinced that, if this had not happened, my life would have turned out differently—maybe for the worse, or for the better. I probably wouldn't be telling this story at all. But my personal passion from that point of change was to break out of the cycle of dependence and to help my parents rise out of poverty too.

My two elder brothers went to secondary school. One finished Form One and the other one completed Form Three. Both dropped out because Father and Mother couldn't pay the school fees. That was the time I didn't believe I would go to secondary school because my parents couldn't raise the fees. However, my Uncle took me to CHES to meet the Agent. She arranged for me to attend Imbale Secondary School, but not on scholarship. I was to prove I could get good marks during that term so I could earn the scholarship. At the end of the term I was the top student, achieving first position in the class, and was awarded the CHES scholarship for the remaining three and a half years.

At the end of Form Two, I was still in first place. I felt I had no competition at Imbale and so I asked CHES for a transfer to attend Form Three and Four in Shikunga Secondary School. There was a small problem there in my choice of elective subjects. Each student had to choose between Agriculture and French. I was not very keen on pursuing Agriculture. The Agent advised me to specialize, firstly, in agriculture and, secondly, in French. I followed her direction, but after a couple of classes I quit Agriculture and opted for French. I soon found out I was trailing the class by two years. Nevertheless, I decided to pursue it with the help of the CHES Agent, who tutored me for a couple of months in order that I could catch up with rest of the students. Unbelievably, I managed a distinction in the national French examinations at the end of secondary school. I was one of the best in French in the entire Western Province and in the government examinations of 1997 I was the student with the best marks in the school.

I believe that during my secondary school years, my life evolved towards success. When I joined Form One, I knew, in my heart, I had a bright future. I had already realized if you lived in Kenya, education was the way to climb the ladder of success out of the pit of poverty in which most Kenyans found themselves. When I finished the fourth form of secondary school, I knew I could do well. A sense of confidence developed inside of me.

After completing secondary school, I taught French and Mathematics at Shikonga Secondary School for the next two years. Teaching made the time productive as I waited out the gap years before I could start university. I also applied to A.C.C.E.S. for a scholarship for university, which couldn't be confirmed until I received my placement.

At the end of that time, with my high academic secondary school achievement, I was selected for Engineering at the University of Nairobi. I was disappointed with the placement and so were my parents. They had wanted me to go into Medicine ever since they had an inkling that I would go to university. Independently, I made up my mind to switch from engineering, and so I did some soul searching about what I wanted to do in my life. I concluded I wanted to work and assist people. That led me to the options of law or medicine. When I tried to switch from the engineering programme, I could only transfer to law. To my mind, going into the law was not merely becoming a professional person. For me, it entailed learning about life and people. I wanted to work with people and in countries where people didn't know their rights. I had seen police brutality and people languishing in jail because they had no knowledge of their rights. I realized they needed legal help. I saw I could assist them and be useful in a good cause. Within the first month I was accepted into Law and finished the four-year programme in 2003.

While I went to university, I was very involved in the Alumni Association of A.C.C.E.S., which the graduate students called C.A.A.A., and was on the executive as the President until December, 2003. I was also very involved in two clubs at the University of Nairobi—the Student Club of Law and Diplomacy, which is like a model United Nations programme, and the Moot Court Club. In my second year I started preparing cases with two of my friends for the Moot Court and by my third year I participated in the East African Moot Court competition on humanitarian law. The stakes were high. I knew that we had to be exceptional to win. Some thought the University of Nairobi team was dominating the competition by winning last year and so we would be assessed more severely this time. In the end, we did win at the finals in South Africa.

That success spurred me to participate more in the Moot Court Club. Through that involvement, I realized I had abilities in presenting law cases. Perhaps, until now, all I had lacked were the opportunities to show my strengths. As opposed to my relatively quiet and introverted demeanour, I came across in the Moot Court situation as very combative and passionate. This surprised many people who knew me and had seen me perform. Though not confrontational, I was very enthusiastic on the floor.

Mooting is basically an art, a drama in reality. It combines a vast knowledge of the law and the factual situation with a person's ability to articulate this knowledge with fluency and style. It is equally vital that one is able to think on their feet, as well as being very agile in thinking and speaking. Many times a person has to be cunning in the manner of the way one responds to the impromptu questions from combative judges. Their questions can sometimes be very vexing. I think that Moot Court is a situation that tests one's balance in many aspects of life. Most importantly, a lawyer-in-training never wants to lose his or her cool on the floor of the court.

In May 2003, after preliminary selection rounds, I was chosen as the Head 'Pleader', representing the University of Nairobi at the All-African Moot Court competition in the Cameroons. At the competition in August 2003, apart from my university being named the best Anglophone team, I was voted the best Oralist of the competition in the Anglophone section—out of one hundred students representing about fifty law faculties. By this achievement, I became the only student from the University of Nairobi and, indeed, Kenya to have won this prestigious individual prize in the competition's twelve year history.

The Moot Court, in Arusha, firmed my passion in human rights. My achievements in all the Moot Court competitions have earned me the scholarship to complete my Masters of Law in Human Rights at the University of Pretoria, in South Africa. I decided to postpone my one-year of internship in Nairobi until after I finish my Masters' programme.

International criminal law and general criminal law are the areas in which I am keenly interested. I have already done some criminal law cases and I like all aspects of them. I am intrigued by criminal law because I may be of use to our society in which many ills abound and, particularly, to my people back home. In a society where it is not suffi-ciently appreciated by those in power that all people have human rights, it will always be imperative there be people ready to put their necks on the line. I know in Kenya great leaders, like Tom Mboya and Jim Kariuki, who did not relent in their agitation for the rights of citizens eventually fell from an assassin's bullet.

Personally, I am going through a rough patch now. I lost my Mother in May, 2003. It pained me a lot. What I am in every present moment is due to my Mother. She was a shining light of what a mother should be. She is everything to me. I am still getting used to her not being there. It is so hard. She was to me the ideal mother and parent. She wanted us kids to succeed. She worked and lived for this. At times, when we thought our Father could have done better than he did for us as a Father, she was always the quiet, uncomplaining woman. In truth, she made all the important decisions in our family. My Mother was the 'hands-on' kind of person.

There are many ways I think I resemble my Mother. She was the kind of person who was little on talk and large in real action. I remember how happy she was when I passed my secondary exams. For the first time I realized how important my success meant to her. Through her quiet modeling, I learned to respect older people and to keep them safe.

We saw each other rarely in the last years of her life because I was away at university in Nairobi, while she took care of our home in the country. I only saw her when I was visiting on business. I always longed for those times when I went home to my Mother. I am still getting used to her not being there. It is so hard.

Because I am the only person in my family at university, I feel the future of my family depends on me. When I am in bed at night, I think that if I fail, I will fail my family. That is why I have always been driven by a need to excel. It is why I have always been the top of my classes. I feel so responsible to look after myself and to help my family and my society. I believe a good lawyer has a major role in society. A lawyer becomes an example of what is good in our society. Lawyers are the voice of the people. There are many signs that a country, like Kenya, emerging from forty years of mis-rule, needs changes in the areas of human rights and administration of justice. Kenya needs good lawyers now—lawyers with a certain sense of responsibility and justice as their guiding principle. Kenya also needs a legal aid program. At present, if a person is charged with a bailable offence, he or she must stay in jail because of not being able to pay the bail or not knowing the law. I want to be of assistance to those types of people. Support and goodwill have been given to me. I feel I have a duty to extend that goodwill to others in need.

In the future I hope to start a foundation of my own to help to educate others. I have been experimenting with that dream in my work with the A.C.C.E.S. Alumni's plan for a savings and loans programme. With time and guidance, our Alumni will reveal what it can do. I want to help in that process.

My passion, outside of law, is reading philosophy, especially Plato, Aristotle, and classical literature. When I studied Engineering at the start of university before I changed into Law, I was introduced to Philosophy as a common course. I began to make meaning out of the small things in life that often pass as mundane. I felt my mind open to new ideas. I must admit I have become more critical because of this philosophical journey. I talked to my friends at university about the ideas, questions and topics that emerged from my readings and courses. My room at the university residence was often the centre of intellectual discussion and discourse. I had some great friends with whom I spent really stimulating times. This is one aspect of university I greatly miss. There are not many people who get interested in asking those vital questions about life and existence.

I write poetry, often of the romantic slant. If I lived in Victor Hugo's time, I would definitely be a Romantic. I really like the French writers— Victor Hugo, Gustave Flaubert, Beaudelaire, Jean Paul Sartre—and certain of the English ones—Shelley, Andrew Marvel, Wordsworth and John Keats. I like the richness of classical literature. Plus I enjoy reading history, biographies and autobiographies. Reading the great writers inspires me, directs my mind on how I should behave and how I should conduct my life. Their thoughts light up my mind.

From my readings, I have found what Africa is experiencing right now has similarities to the French Revolution. For the last forty years, Kenyans have lived through a similar plunder and rot that formed the justification for the French revolution over two hundred years ago. Kenya has been lucky to escape the sad wars that the African continent has seen for many years. A different kind of war has been waged in Kenya. It has been a war of economic plunder, mismanagement and impoverishment of the masses. It is a war that has decimated all, if not most, of the institutions of society and crushed the hopes of the masses. It can be said now that we were on our last legs just before the last elections in December, 2002. It is a wonder that our country, after such rigorous years, was able to maintain any muscle at all. If it had not been for these years of waste, Kenya could be one of the richest countries on the continent. Currently, Kenya is at a crossroads."

We finished the interview taping at that point. Over a year passed. I was on the final stages of my writing when Godfrey sent me an email which sang with achievements:

"I graduated as the best student in the Master of Law class and I was really pleasantly surprised about this. As a result I got the Nelson Mandela Prize for the best overall student and the Keba M'baye Prize for the best thesis. I, also, am so elated about some good news I received five days ago. I have secured a fully funded internship of six months with the United Nations International Tribunal of Rwanda, in Arusha, Tanzania. This role is particularly important for me because it seems I am starting out on a path I have so much wanted to follow—international criminal law. I know if I work at it, I can be the best international lawyer that I can be. I figure I am one lucky guy. I'll keep you posted on any further developments.

I realize I have not done much. Yet!"

Godfrey Musila

A quiet and thoughtful man,

Of incredible intellect and ambition.

Passionate about law and human rights,

Driven to success by his past and a sense of responsibility

To be a human rights lawyer.

Extraordinary orator in court.

Literate, philosophical and well-read,

A leader for future change.

Concluding Notes

*W*hen I returned to Vancouver from Kenya in October 2003, I had only begun to understand the complexities in the lives of these twelve men and women. All but one had started life in a peasant family in rural Western Kenya where poverty and lack of opportunity to be educated entrenched most youth in the traditional ways of past generations. Each person I interviewed had been given a Canadian-donated A.C.C.E.S. scholarship for a university or college education which opened the door to a new way of living in modern Kenya. Most had previously received a secondary school scholarship from A.C.C.E.S.' sister organization, CHES.

However, as I interviewed and inter-acted with these men and women, I began to understand the qualities of a person which would lead to a successful new life after years of poverty. The majority of these twelve men and women have incredible intellectual abilities that set them apart from other students. Each also demonstrates specific personal strengths: Cappitus' persistence to attend school, Davis' flexibility to use any opportunity creatively, Margaret's determination to excel, and Justine's passion to make a difference to the scourge of AIDS that was devastating his town. These are only some of the characteristics that facilitated change in their lives.

But the opportunity to be funded through university or college also made them realize that their future could be different. The annual scholarship given by ordinary people in faraway British Columbia, Canada, opened the door for each Kenyan to change his or her life, going on to complete the cycle of giving by assisting others in their family. In getting to know each of these young men and women, I have grown optimistic about the future of Kenya.

My hope is this book will ignite an understanding that education is the key to develop Kenyans. Education will help them set the future course of their country. A homespun Canadian organization, A.C.C.E.S., founded on this belief in 1993 by George and Beth Scott, has slowly and surely advanced the cycle of change and the concept of sustainability in the large western province of Kenya over the past twelve years. With A.C.C.E.S' help, some Kenyans are now leading extraordinary lives of change. The power of education has been revealed to Kenyans and to their Canadian sponsors.

These young Kenyans are so committed to the A.C.C.E.S. philosophy that they shared their stories so the proceeds from the sale of this book go to the A.C.C.E.S. scholarship fund. Thus, other young, bright, but poor men and women will be educated. Their extraordinary lives continue to light the way to Kenya's future.

PHOTO COURTESY M. MacDONALD

There are many ways to become involved and support the work of ACCES:

→ Visit **www.acceskenya.org** to learn more about programs, annual reports, volunteer opportunities and upcoming events.

→ Sign up for the monthly ACCES update email, which features a story from the field, a brief news update and upcoming events. To register, write to: **info@acceskenya.org**

→ Sign up for the biannual newsletter for more in-depth stories and photos about the work and people of ACCES. Send your address to **info@acceskenya.org** or the mailing address below.

→ Make a donation. All donations are tax-deductible in Canada and the USA (note: U.S. citizens should contact us for details), and 100% of funds designated for programs go directly to those programs. Donations can be made:

1. Online at **www.acceskenya.org**
2. Through United Way payroll deductions
3. By cheque - please fill in the form below

❑ $400: Sponsorship of one post-secondary student for one year

❑ $100: Vitamins for one primary school class for one year

❑ $45: Teaching supplies for one classroom for one year

❑ $_____: to support ACCES

_____

NAME

_____

ADDRESS

_____

CITY   PROVINCE/STATE   POSTAL CODE/ZIP

_____

EMAIL (for monthly email update – ACCES does not ever share addresses)

Mail to:

ACCES
2441 Christopherson Road
Surrey, BC Canada V4A 3L2

About the Author

Born in Ontario, Canada, Sandra Harper has filled her life with family and friends, an educational career, followed by a new career in writing and traveling the world. She has a PhD. from Bradford University, England, which focused on assessing how people change when faced with an innovation. In May 2004, she published her first book, *Traveling the Sun: A Healing Journey in Morocco, Tunisia and Spain.* While she was writing this book, she spent six months during 2003 in Kakamega, Kenya, as a volunteer for A.C.C.E.S. While in Kenya, the idea for *Inside Kenya – Creating Tomorrow* was born. She lives in Vancouver, British Columbia, when she is home from her various journeys.

Selected Books to Consult

There are many books on Kenya. The books I have referred to are the books that have profoundly affected me as I wrote this book. They are exceptional portrayals of the Kenya I came to know and love. There are many more books that are worthy and recommended for those who want to learn more, but space is limited.

Achebe, Chinua. *Things Fall Apart.* New York: Anchor Books, 1994.

Achebe, Chinua *et al. Encounters from Africa.* Nairobi: Macmillan, 2000.

Achebe, Chinua and Lyons, Robert. *Another Africa.* Nairobi: East African Educational Publishers, 1998.

Conteh, Falmatah *et al. Half A Day and Other Stories.* Nairobi: Macmillan Kenya Publishers, 2004.

Gates, Henry Louis Jr. *Wonders of the African World.* New York: Random House, 1999.

Kenyatta, Jomo. *Facing Mount Kenya.* Nairobi: Kenway Publication, 1938.

Lamb, David. *The Africans.* New York: Random House, 1983.

Mandella, Nelson. *Long Walk to Freedom.* New York: Little, Brown and Company, 1994.

Mboya, Tom. *The Challenge of Nationhood.* Nairobi: East African Educational Publishers, 1993.

Murphy, Dervla. *The Ukimwi Road: From Kenya to Zimbabwe.* London: Flamingo, 1993.

Ogot, Grace. *The Promised Land.* Nairobi: East African Educational Publishers, 1966.

Pavitt, Nigel. *Africa's Great Rift Valley.* New York: Harry N. Abrams, 2001.

Stackhouse, John. *Out of Poverty.* Toronto: Vintage Canada, 2001.